Modern Critical Interpretations

Charles Dickens's
Bleak House

Modern Critical Interpretations

These and other titles in preparation

Modern Critical Interpretations

Charles Dickens's
Bleak House

Edited and with an introduction by

Harold Bloom
Sterling Professor of the Humanities
Yale University

Chelsea House Publishers ◊ *1987*

NEW YORK ◊ **NEW HAVEN** ◊ **PHILADELPHIA**

© 1987 by Chelsea House Publishers, a division
of Chelsea House Educational Communications, Inc.,
   95 Madison Avenue, New York, NY 10016
   345 Whitney Avenue, New Haven, CT 06511
   5014 West Chester Pike, Edgemont, PA 19028

Introduction © 1987 by Harold Bloom

Printed and bound in the United States of America

∞ The paper used in this publication meets the minimum
requirements of the American National Standard for
Permanence of Paper for Printed Library Materials,
Z39.48–1984.

Library of Congress Cataloging-in-Publication Data
Charles Dickens's Bleak house.
   (Modern critical interpretations)
   Bibliography: p.
   Includes index.
   1. Dickens, Charles, 1812–1870. Bleak house.
I. Bloom, Harold.   II. Series.
PR4556.C48   1987   823'.8   86-33465
ISBN 0-87754-735-1 (alk. paper)

Contents

Editor's Note

This book gathers together a representative selection of the best criticism available upon *Bleak House,* generally regarded now as Charles Dickens's greatest work. The critical essays are reprinted here in the chronological sequence of their original publication. I am grateful to Guy Moppel for his aid in researching this volume.

My introduction seeks to relate what John Ruskin called Dickens's mastery of "stage fire" to the apocalyptic elements in *Bleak House.* J. Hillis Miller, who seems to me the most eminent of living Dickens critics, begins the chronological sequence of commentary with an overt deconstruction in which he attempts to show that: "The situation of characters within the novel corresponds to the situation of its reader or author."

Esther Summerson, perhaps the most critically maligned of all central characters in Dickens, is rehabilitated by Alex Zwerdling as an instance of "detailed psychological realism," and by Judith Wilt as a representation of the novelist's triumphant projection of himself into the fictive consciousness of a woman.

Garrett Stewart studies the function of chapter titles in *Bleak House* as signs of "death's aesthetic utility, its cruel beauty." The novel's conclusion is examined by John Kucich, who finds in it Esther's victory over Lady Dedlock's muddle, which is a version of the death drive that Esther has refused to repeat. Christopher Herbert, meditating upon the occult in *Bleak House,* uncovers the shape of "Dickens's intuition that beneath the surface of 'familiar things' in modern England lies a maelstrom of occult apparitions."

In this volume's final essay, Virginia Blain approaches the novel from a professedly feminist perspective and faults it for its own version of the male double standard in regard to female power, sexuality, and supposed guilt. I do not believe that Dickens would have accepted Blain's judgment that Esther "is rewarded for having purged her mother's sexual taint," but Blain has raised matters that are part of the legitimate burden of an ongoing feminist criticism.

Introduction

Courage would be the critical virtue most required if anyone were to attempt an essay that might be called "The Limitations of Shakespeare." Tolstoy, in his most outrageous critical performance, more or less tried just that, with dismal results, and even Ben Jonson might not have done much better, had he sought to extend his ambivalent *obiter dicta* on his great friend and rival. Nearly as much courage, or foolhardiness, is involved in discoursing on the limitations of Dickens, but the young Henry James had a critical gusto that could carry him through every literary challenge. Reviewing *Our Mutual Friend* in 1865, James exuberantly proclaimed that "*Bleak House* was forced; *Little Dorrit* was labored; the present work is dug out as with a spade and pickaxe." At about this time, reviewing *Drum-Taps,* James memorably dismissed Whitman as an essentially prosaic mind seeking to lift itself, by muscular exertion, into poetry. To reject some of the major works of the strongest English novelist and the greatest American poet, at about the same moment, is to set standards for critical audacity that no one since has been able to match, even as no novelist since has equalled Dickens, nor any poet, Walt Whitman.

James was at his rare worst in summing up Dickens's supposedly principal inadequacy:

> Such scenes as this are useful in fixing the limits of Mr. Dickens's insight. Insight is, perhaps, too strong a word; for we are convinced that it is one of the chief conditions of his genius not to see beneath the surface of things. If we might hazard a definition of his literary character, we should, accordingly, call him the greatest of superficial novelists. We are aware that this definition confines him to an inferior rank

1

in the department of letters which he adorns; but we accept this consequence of our proposition. It were, in our opinion, an offence against humanity to place Mr. Dickens among the greatest novelists. For, to repeat what we have already intimated, he has created nothing but figure. He has added nothing to our understanding of human character. He is master of but two alternatives: he reconciles us to what is commonplace, and he reconciles us to what is odd. The value of the former service is questionable; and the manner in which Mr. Dickens performs it sometimes conveys a certain impression of charlatanism. The value of the latter service is incontestable, and here Mr. Dickens is an honest, an admirable artist.

This can be taken literally, and then transvalued: to see truly the surface of things, to reconcile us at once to the commonplace and the odd—these are not minor gifts. In 1860, John Ruskin, the great seer of the surface of things, the charismatic illuminator of the commonplace and the odd together, had reached a rather different conclusion from that of the young Henry James five years before James's brash rejection:

> The essential value and truth of Dickens's writings have been unwisely lost sight of by many thoughtful persons merely because he presents his truth with some colour of caricature. Unwisely, because Dickens's caricature, though often gross, is never mistaken. Allowing for his manner of telling them, the things he tells us are always true. I wish that he could think it right to limit his brilliant exaggeration to works written only for public amusement; and when he takes up a subject of high national importance, such as that which he handled in *Hard Times,* that he would use severer and more accurate analysis. The usefulness of that work (to my mind, in several respects, the greatest he has written) is with many persons seriously diminished because Mr. Bounderby is a dramatic monster, instead of a characteristic example of a worldly master; and Stephen Blackpool a dramatic perfection, instead of a characteristic example of an honest workman. But let us not lose the use of Dickens's wit and insight, because he chooses to speak in a circle of stage fire. He is entirely right in his main drift and purpose in every book he has written; and all of them,

but especially *Hard Times,* should be studied with close and earnest care by persons interested in social questions. They will find much that is partial, and, because partial, apparently unjust; but if they examine all the evidence on the other side, which Dickens seems to overlook, it will appear, after all their trouble, that his view was the finally right one, grossly and sharply told.

To say of Dickens that he chose "to speak in a circle of stage fire" is exactly right, since Dickens is the greatest actor among novelists, the finest master of dramatic projection. A superb stage performer, he never stops performing in his novels, which is not the least of his many Shakespearean characteristics. Martin Price usefully defines some of these as "his effortless invention, his brilliant play of language, the scope and density of his imagined world." I like also Price's general comparison of Dickens to the strongest satirist in the language, Swift, a comparison that Price shrewdly turns into a confrontation:

> But the confrontation helps us to define differences as well: Dickens is more explicit, more overtly compassionate, insisting always upon the perversions of feeling as well as of thought. His outrage is of the same consistency as his generous celebration, the satirical wit of the same copious extravagance as the comic elaborations. Dickens's world is alive with things that snatch, lurch, teeter, thrust, leer; it is the animate world of Netherlandish genre painting or of Hogarth's prints, where all space is a field of force, where objects vie or intrigue with each other, where every human event spills over into the things that surround it. This may become the typically crowded scene of satire, where persons are reduced to things and things to matter in motion; or it may pulsate with fierce energy and noisy feeling. It is different from Swift; it is the distinctive Dickensian plenitude, which we find again in his verbal play, in his great array of vivid characters, in his massed scenes of feasts or public declamations. It creates rituals as compelling as the resuscitation of Rogue Riderhood, where strangers participate solemnly in the recovery of a spark of life, oblivious for the moment of the unlovely human form it will soon inhabit.

That animate, Hogarthian world, "where all space is a field of force," indeed is a plenitude and it strikes me that Price's vivid description suggests Rabelais rather than Swift as a true analogue. Dickens, like Shakespeare in one of many aspects and like Rabelais, is as much carnival as stage fire, a kind of endless festival. The reader of Dickens stands in the midst of a festival, which is too varied, too multiform, to be taken in even by innumerable readings. Something always escapes our ken; Ben Jonson's sense of being "rammed with life" is exemplified more even by Dickens than by Rabelais, in that near-Shakespearean plenitude that is Dickens's peculiar glory.

Is it possible to define that plenitude narrowly enough so as to conceptualize it for critical use, though by "conceptualize" one meant only a critical metaphor? Shakespearean representation is no touch-stone for Dickens or for anyone else, since above all modes of representation it turns upon an inward changing brought about by characters listening to themselves speak. Dickens cannot do that. His villains are gorgeous, but there are no Iagos or Edmunds among them. The severer, more relevant test, which Dickens must fail, though hardly to his detriment, is Falstaff, who generates not only his own meaning, but meaning in so many others besides, both on and off the page. Probably the severest test is Shylock, most Dickensian of Shakespeare's characters, since we cannot say of Dickens's Shylock, Fagin, that there is much Shakespearean about him at all. Fagin is a wonderful grotesque, but the winds of will are not stirred in him, while they burn on hellishly forever in Shylock.

Carlyle's injunction, to work in the will, seems to have little enough place in the cosmos of the Dickens characters. I do not say this to indicate a limitation, or even a limit, nor do I believe that the will to live or the will to power is ever relaxed in or by Dickens. But nothing is got for nothing, except perhaps in or by Shakespeare, and Dickens purchases his kind of plenitude at the expense of one aspect of the will. T. S. Eliot remarked that "Dickens's characters are real because there is no one like them." I would modify that to "They are real because they are not like one another, though sometimes they are a touch more like some of us than like each other." Perhaps the will, in whatever aspect, can differ only in degree rather than in kind among us. The aesthetic secret of Dickens appears to be that his villains, heroes, heroines, victims, eccentrics, ornamental beings, do differ from one another *in the kinds of will that they possess*. Since that is hardly possible for us, as humans, it does bring about an absence in reality in and for Dickens. That is a high price to pay, but it is a good deal less than everything and Dickens got more than he paid for. We also receive a great deal more than we ever are asked to surrender when we read Dickens. That may indeed be his most Shakespearean quality, and may provide the critical trope I quest for in him. James and Proust hurt you more than Dickens does, and the hurt is the meaning, or much of it. What hurts in Dickens never has much to do with meaning, because there cannot be a poetics of pain where the will has ceased to be common or sadly uniform. Dickens really does offer a poetics of pleasure, which is surely worth our secondary uneasiness at his refusal to offer us any accurately mimetic representations of the human will. He writes always the book of the drives, which is why supposedly Freudian readings of him always fail so tediously. The conceptual metaphor he suggests in his representations of character and personality is neither Shakespearean mirror nor Romantic lamp, neither Rabelaisian carnival nor Fieldingesque open country. "Stage fire" seems to me perfect, for "stage" removes something of the reality of the will, yet only as modifier. The substantive remains "fire." Dickens is the poet of the fire of the drives, the true celebrant of Freud's myth of frontier concepts, of that domain lying on the border between psyche and body, falling into matter, yet partaking of the reality of both.

II

Bleak House may not be "the finest literary work the nineteenth century produced in England," as Geoffrey Tillotson called it in 1946. A century that gave us *The Prelude* and Wordsworth's major crisis lyrics, Blake's *Milton* and *Jerusalem*, Byron's *Don Juan*, the principal poems of Shelley, Keats, Tennyson, and Browning, and novels such as *Pride and Prejudice, Emma, Middlemarch,* and Dickens's own *Hard Times* and *Our Mutual Friend*, is an era of such literary plenitude that a single choice is necessarily highly problematic. Yet there is now something close to critical agreement that *Bleak House* is Dickens's most complex and memorable single achievement. W. J. Harvey usefully sketches just how formidably the novel is patterned:

> *Bleak House* is for Dickens a unique and elaborate experiment in narration and plot composition. It is divided into two intermingled and roughly concurrent stories; Esther Summerson's first-person narrative and an omniscient narrative told consistently in the historic present. The latter takes up thirty-four chapters; Esther has one less. Her story,

however, occupies a good deal more than half the novel. The reader who checks the distribution of these two narratives against the original part issues will hardly discern any significant pattern or correlation. Most parts contain a mixture of the two stories; one part is narrated entirely by Esther and five parts entirely by the omniscient author. Such a check does, however, support the view that Dickens did not, as is sometimes supposed, use serial publication in the interest of crude suspense. A sensational novelist, for example, might well have ended a part issue with chapter 31; Dickens subdues the drama by adding another chapter to the number. The obvious exception to this only proves the rule; in the final double number the suspense of Bucket's search for Lady Dedlock is heightened by cutting back to the omniscient narrative and the stricken Sir Leicester. In general, however, Dickens's control of the double narrative is far richer and subtler than this.

I would add to Harvey the critical observation that Dickens's own narrative will in "his" thirty-four chapters is a will again different in kind from the will to tell her story of the admirable Esther Summerson. Dickens's (or the omniscient, historical present narrator's) metaphor of representation is one of "stage fire": wild, free, unconditioned, incessant with the force of Freud's domain of those grandly indefinite frontier concepts, the drives. Esther's mode of representation is certainly not flat or insipid; for all of her monumental repressions, Esther finally seems to me the most mysteriously complex and profound personage in *Bleak House*. Her narrative is not so much plain style as it is indeed repressed in the precise Freudian sense of "repression," whose governing metaphor, in Esther's prose as in Freud's, is flight from, rather than a pushing down or pushing under. Esther frequently forgets, purposefully though "unconsciously," what she cannot bear to remember, and much of her narrative is her strong defense against the force of the past. Esther may not *appear* to change as she goes from little girl to adult, but that is because the rhythm of her psyche, unlike Dickens's own, is one of unfolding rather than development. She is Dickens's Muse, what Whitman would have called his "Fancy," as in the great death-lyric "Good-bye, my Fancy!" or what Stevens would have called Dickens's "Interior Paramour."

Contrast a passage of Esther's story with one of Dickens's own narrative, from the end of chapter 56, "Pursuit," and toward the close of the next chapter, "Esther's Narrative":

> Mr. Jarndyce, the only person up in the house, is just going to bed; rises from his book, on hearing the rapid ringing at the bell; and comes down to the door in his dressing-gown.
>
> "Don't be alarmed sir." In a moment his visitor is confidential with him in the hall, has shut the door, and stands with his hand upon the lock. "I've had the pleasure of seeing you before. Inspector Bucket. Look at that handkerchief, sir, Miss Esther Summerson's. Found it myself put away in a drawer of Lady Dedlock's, quarter of an hour ago. Not a moment to lose. Matter of life or death. You know Lady Dedlock?"
>
> "Yes."
>
> "There has been a discovery there, to-day. Family affairs have come out. Sir Leicester Dedlock, Baronet, has had a fit—apoplexy or paralysis—and couldn't be brought to, and precious time has been lost. Lady Dedlock disappeared this afternoon, and left a letter for him that looks bad. Run your eye over it. Here it is!"
>
> Mr. Jarndyce having read it, asks him what he thinks?
>
> "I don't know. It looks like suicide. Anyways, there's more and more danger, every minute, of its drawing to that. I'd give a hundred pound an hour to have got the start of the present time. Now, Mr. Jarndyce, I am employed by Sir Leicester Dedlock, Baronet, to follow her and find her—to save her, and take her his forgiveness. I have money and full power, but I want something else. I want Miss Summerson."
>
> Mr. Jarndyce, in a troubled voice, repeats "Miss Summerson?"
>
> "Now, Mr. Jarndyce"; Mr. Bucket has read his face with the greatest attention all along: "I speak to you as a gentleman of a humane heart, and under such pressing circumstances as don't often happen. If ever delay was dangerous, it's dangerous now; and if ever you couldn't afterwards forgive yourself for causing it, this is the time. Eight or ten hours, worth, as I tell you, a hundred pound apiece at least, have been lost since Lady Dedlock disap-

peared. I am charged to find her. I am Inspector Bucket. Besides all the rest that's heavy on her, she has upon her, as she believes, suspicion of murder. If I follow her alone, she, being in ignorance of what Sir Leicester Dedlock, Baronet, has communicated to me, may be driven to desperation. But if I follow her in company with a young lady, answering to the description of a young lady that she has a tenderness for—I ask no question, and I say no more than that—she will give me credit for being friendly. Let me come up with her, and be able to have the hold upon her of putting that young lady for'ard, and I'll save her and prevail with her if she is alive. Let me come up with her alone—a harder matter—and I'll do my best; but I don't answer for what the best may be. Time flies; it's getting on for one o'clock. When one strikes, there's another hour gone; and it's worth a thousand pound now, instead of a hundred."

This is all true, and the pressing nature of the case cannot be questioned. Mr. Jarndyce begs him to remain there, while he speaks to Miss Summerson. Mr. Bucket says he will; but acting on his usual principle, does no such thing—following up-stairs instead, and keeping his man in sight. So he remains, dodging and lurking about in the gloom of the staircase while they confer. In a very little time, Mr. Jarndyce comes down, and tells him that Miss Summerson will join him directly, and place herself under his protection, to accompany him where he pleases. Mr. Bucket, satisfied, expresses high approval; and awaits her coming, at the door.

There, he mounts a high tower in his mind, and looks out far and wide. Many solitary figures he perceives, creeping through the streets; many solitary figures out on heaths, and roads, and lying under haystacks. But the figure that he seeks is not among them. Other solitaries he perceives, in nooks of bridges, looking over; and in shadowed places down by the river's level; and a dark, dark, shapeless object drifting with the tide, more solitary than all, clings with a drowning hold on his attention.

Where is she? Living or dead, where is she? If, as he folds the handkerchief and carefully puts it up, it were able, with an enchanted power, to bring before him the place where she found it, and the night landscape near the cottage where it covered the little child, would he descry her there? On the waste, where the brick-kilns are burning with a pale blue flare; where the straw-roofs of the wretched huts in which the bricks are made, are being scattered by the wind; where the clay and water are hard frozen, and the mill in which the gaunt blind horse goes round all day, looks like an instrument of human torture;—traversing this deserted blighted spot, there is a lonely figure with the sad world to itself, pelted by the snow and driven by the wind, and cast out, it would seem, from all companionship. It is the figure of a woman, too; but it is miserably dressed, and no such clothes ever came through the hall, and out at the great door, of the Dedlock mansion.

The transparent windows with the fire and light, looking so bright and warm from the cold darkness out of doors, were soon gone, and again we were crushing and churning the loose snow. We went on with toil enough; but the dismal roads were not much worse than they had been, and the stage was only nine miles. My companion smoking on the box—I had thought at the last inn of begging him to do so, when I saw him standing at a great fire in a comfortable cloud of tobacco—was as vigilant as ever; and as quickly down and up again, when we came to any human abode or any human creature. He had lighted his little dark lantern, which seemed to be a favourite with him, for we had lamps to the carriage; and every now and then he turned it upon me, to see that I was doing well. There was a folding-window to the carriage-head, but I never closed it, for it seemed like shutting out hope.

We came to the end of the stage, and still the lost trace was not recovered. I looked at him anxiously when we stopped to change; but I knew by his yet graver face, as he stood watching the ostlers, that he had heard nothing. Almost in an instant afterwards, as I leaned back in my seat, he looked in, with his lighted lantern in his hand, an excited and quite different man.

"What is it?" said I, starting. "Is she here?"

"No, no. Don't deceive yourself, my dear. Nobody's here. But I've got it!"

The crystallised snow was in his eyelashes, in his hair, lying in ridges on his dress. He had to shake it from his face, and get his breath before he spoke to me.

"Now, Miss Summerson," said he, beating his finger on the apron, "don't you be disappointed at what I'm a going to do. You know me. I'm Inspector Bucket, and you can trust me. We've come a long way; never mind. Four horses out there for the next stage up! Quick!"

There was a commotion in the yard, and a man came running out of the stables to know "if he meant up or down?"

"Up, I tell you! Up! Ain't it English? Up!"

"Up?" said I, astonished. "To London! Are we going back?"

"Miss Summerson," he answered, "back. Straight back as a die. You know me. Don't be afraid. I'll follow the other, by G——."

"The other?" I repeated. "Who?"

"You called her Jenny, didn't you? I'll follow her. Bring those two pair out here, for a crown a man. Wake up, some of you!"

"You will not desert this lady we are in search of; you will not abandon her on such a night, and in such a state of mind as I know her to be in!" said I, in an agony, and grasping his hand.

"You are right, my dear, I won't. But I'll follow the other. Look alive here with them horses. Send a man for'ard in the saddle to the next stage, and let him send another for'ard again, and order four on, up, right through. My darling, don't you be afraid!"

These orders, and the way in which he ran about the yard, urging them, caused a general excitement that was scarcely less bewildering to me than the sudden change. But in the height of the confusion, a mounted man galloped away to order the relays, and our horses were put to with great speed.

"My dear," said Mr. Bucket, jumping up to his seat, and looking in again—"you'll excuse me if I'm too familiar—don't you fret and worry yourself no more than you can help. I say nothing else at present; but you know me, my dear; now, don't you?"

I endeavoured to say that I knew he was far more capable than I of deciding what we ought to do; but was he sure that this was right? Could I not go forward by myself in search of—I grasped his hand again in my distress, and whispered it to him—of my own mother.

"My dear," he answered, "I know, I know, and would I put you wrong, do you think? Inspector Bucket. Now you know me, don't you?"

What could I say but yes!

"Then you keep up as good a heart as you can, and you rely upon me for standing by you, no less than by Sir Leicester Dedlock, Baronet. Now, are you right there?"

"All right, sir!"

"Off she goes, then. And get on, my lads!"

We were again upon the melancholy road by which we had come; tearing up the miry sleet and thawing snow, as if they were torn up by a waterwheel.

Both passages are extraordinary, by any standards, and certainly "Pursuit" has far more stage fire than "Esther's Narrative," but this time her repressive shield, in part, is broken through, and a fire leaps forth out of her. If we start with "Pursuit," however, we are likelier to see what it is that returns from the repressed in Esther, returns under the sign of negation (as Freud prophesied), so that what comes back is primarily cognitive, while the affective aspect of the repression persists. We can remember the opening of *David Copperfield,* where Dickens in his *persona* as David disavows the gift of second sight attributed to him by the wise women and gossips. Inspector Bucket, at the conclusion of the "Pursuit" chapter, is granted a great vision, a preternatural second sight of Esther's lost mother, Lady Dedlock. What Bucket *sees* is stage fire at its most intense, the novelist's will to tell become an absolute vision of the will. Mounting a high tower in his mind, Bucket (who thus becomes Dickens's authorial will) looks out, far and wide, and sees the truth: "a dark, dark, shapeless object drifting with the tide, more solitary than all," which "clings with a drowning hold on his attention." That "drowning hold" leads to the further vision: "where the clay and water are hard frozen, and the mill in which the gaunt blind horse goes round all day." I suspect that Dickens here has a debt to Browning's great romance, "Childe Roland to the Dark Tower Came," where another apparent instrument of human torture in a deserted, blighted spot, is seen by a companionless figure as being in association with a starving blind horse, cast out from the Devil's stud, who provokes in Browning's narrator the terrible outcry that he never saw a beast he hated so, because: "He must be wicked to deserve such pain."

The ensuing chapter of "Esther's Narrative" brilliantly evokes the cognitive return of Esther's acknowledgment of her mother, under the sign of a negation of past affect. Here the narrative vision proceeds, not in the sublime mode of Bucket's extraordinary second sight, but in the grave, meditative lyricism that takes us first to a tentative return from unconscious flight through an image of pursuit of the fleeing, doomed mother: "The transparent windows with the fire and light, looking so bright and warm from the cold darkness out of doors, were soon gone, and again we were crushing and churning the loose snow." That "crushing and churning" images the breaking of the repressive shield, and Dickens shrewdly ends the chapter with Esther's counterpart to Bucket's concluding vision of a Browningesque demonic water mill, torturing consciousness into a return from flight. Esther whispers to Bucket that she desires to go forward by herself in search of her own mother, and the dark pursuit goes on in the sinister metaphor of the sleet and thawing snow, shield of repression, being torn up by a waterwheel that recirculates the meaning of memory's return, even as it buries part of the pains of abandonment by the mother once more: "We were again upon the melancholy road by which we had come; tearing up the miry sleet and thawing snow, as if they were torn up by a waterwheel."

It is a terrifying triumph of Dickens's art that, when "Esther's Narative" resumes, in chapter 59, we know inevitably that we are headed straight for an apocalyptic image of what Shakespeare, in *King Lear,* calls "the promised end" or "image of that horror," here not the corpse of the daughter, but of the mother. Esther goes, as she must, to be the first to touch and to see, and with no affect whatsoever, unveils the truth:

> I passed on to the gate, and stooped down. I lifted the heavy head, put the long dank hair aside, and turned the face. And it was my mother, cold and dead.

The Interpretive Dance
in *Bleak House*

J. Hillis Miller

forcing, adjusting, abbreviating, omitting, padding, inventing,
falsifying, and whatever else is of the essence *of interpreting*
NIETZSCHE, *On the Genealogy of Morals*

Bleak House is a document about the interpretation of documents. Like many great works of literature it raises questions about its own status as a text. The novel doubles back on itself or turns itself inside out. The situation of characters within the novel corresponds to the situation of its reader or author.

In writing *Bleak House* Dickens constructed a model in little of English society in his time. In no other of his novels is the canvas broader, the sweep more inclusive, the linguistic and dramatic texture richer, the gallery of comic grotesques more extraordinary. As other critics have shown (most notably John Butt and Kathleen Tillotson in "The Topicality of *Bleak House*" [*Dickens at Work*] and Humphry House in "*Bleak House:* The Time Scale" [*The Dickens World*]), the novel accurately reflects the social reality of Dickens's day, in part of the time of publication in 1851–53, in part of the time of Dickens's youth, in the late twenties, when he was a reporter in the Lord Chancellor's court. The scandal of the Court of Chancery, sanitary reform, slum clearance, orphans' schools, the recently formed detective branch of the Metropolitan Police Force, Puseyite philanthropists, the Niger expedition, female emancipation, the self-

From *Bleak House,* edited by Norman Paige with an introduction by J. Hillis Miller. © 1971 by Penguin Books Ltd.

perpetuating procrastinations of Parliament and Government—each is represented in some character or scene. Every detail of topography or custom has its journalistic correspondence to the reality of Dickens's time. Everything mirrors some fact—from the exact references to street names and localities—mostly, it has been noted, within half a mile of Chancery Lane—to the "copying" of Leigh Hunt and Walter Savage Landor in Skimpole and Boythorn, to such out-of-the-way details as the descriptions of a shooting gallery, a law stationer's shop, or the profession of "follower." Like Dickens's first book, *Sketches by Boz, Bleak House* is in imitation in words of the culture of a city.

The means of this mimesis is synecdoche. In *Bleak House* each character, scene, or situation stands for innumerable other examples of a given type. Mrs Pardiggle is the model of a Puseyite philanthropist; Mrs Jellyby of another sort of irresponsible do-gooder; Mr Vholes of the respectable solicitor battening on victims of Chancery; Tulkinghorn of the lawyer to great families; Gridley, Miss Flite, Ada and Richard of different sorts of Chancery suitors; Mr Chadband of the hypocritical Evangelical clergyman mouthing distorted Biblical language; Bucket of the detective policeman, one of the first great examples in literature; Jo of the homeless poor; Tom-all-Alone's of urban slums in general; Sir Leicester Dedlock of the conservative aristocracy; Chesney Wold of the country homes of such men. Nor is the reader left to identify the representative quality of these personages for himself. The narrator constantly calls the reader's attention to their ecumenical role. For each Chadband, Mrs Pardiggle, Jo, Chesney Wold or Gridley there are many more similar cases. Each example has its idiosyncrasies (who but Chadband could be just like Chadband?), but the essence of the type remains the same.

Bleak House is a model of English society in yet another way. The network of relations among the various characters is a miniature version of the interconnectedness of people in all levels of society. From Jo the crossing-sweeper to Sir Leicester Dedlock in his country estate, all Englishmen, in Dickens's view, are members of one family. The Dedlock mystery and the case of Jarndyce and Jarndyce bring all the characters together in unforeseen ways. This bringing together creates a web of connection from which no character is free. The narrator formulates the law of this interdependence in two questions, the first in reference to this particular story and the second in reference to all the stories of which this story is representative:

What connexion can there be, between the place in Lincolnshire, the house in town, the Mercury in powder, and the whereabout of Jo the outlaw with the broom, who had that distant ray of light upon him when he swept the churchyard-step? What connexion can there have been between many people in the innumerable histories of this world, who, from opposite sides of great gulfs, have, nevertheless, been very curiously brought together!

In the emblematic quality of the characters and of their "connexions" *Bleak House* is an interpretation of Victorian society. This is so in more than one sense. As a blueprint is an image in another form of the building for which it is the plan, so *Bleak House* transfers England into another realm, the realm of fictional language. This procedure of synecdochic transference, naming one thing in terms of another, is undertaken as a means of investigation. Dickens wants to define England exactly and to identify exactly the causes of its present state. As everyone knows, he finds England in a bad way. It is in a state dangerously close to ultimate disorder or decay. The energy which gave the social system its initial impetus seems about to run down. Entropy approaches a maximum. Emblems of this perilous condition abound in *Bleak House*—the fog and mud of its admirable opening, the constant rain at Chesney Wold, the spontaneous combustion of Krook, the ultimate consumption in costs of the Jarndyce estate, the deaths of so many characters in the course of the novel (I count nine).

With description goes explanation. Dickens wants to tell how things got as they are, to indict someone for the crime. Surely it cannot be, in the phrase he considered as a title for *Little Dorrit,* "Nobody's Fault." Someone must be to blame. There must be steps to take to save England before it blows up, like the springing of a mine, or catches fire, like Krook, or falls in fragments, like the houses in Tom-all-Alone's, or resolves into dust, which awaits all men and all social systems. It is not easy, however, to formulate briefly the results of Dickens's interpretative act. His two spokesmen, the narrators, are engaged in a search. This search brings a revelation of secrets and leads the reader to expect an explanation of their meaning. The novel as a whole is the narrators' reports on what they have seen, but these can only be understood by means of a further interpretation—the reader's.

Bleak House does not easily yield its meaning. Its significance is by no means transparent. Both narrators hide as much as they reveal. The habitual method of the novel is to present persons and scenes which are conspicuously enigmatic. The reader is invited in various ways to read the signs, to decipher the mystery. This invitation is made openly by the anonymous, present-tense narrator through rhetorical questions and other devices of language. The invitation to interpret is performed more covertly by Esther Summerson in her past-tense narrative. Her pretence not to understand the dishonesty, hypocrisy or self-deception of the people she encounters, though she gives the reader the information necessary to understand them, is such an invitation, as is her coy withholding of information which she has at the time she writes, but did not have at the time she has reached in her story: "I did not understand it. Not for many and many a day."

Moreover, the narrators offer here and there examples of the proper way to read the book. They encourage the reader to consider the names, gestures and appearances of the characters as indications of some hidden truth about them. Esther, for example, in spite of her reluctance to read signs, says that Prince Turveydrop's "little innocent, feminine manner" "made this singular effect upon me: that I received the impression that he was like his mother, and that his mother had not been much considered or well used." The anonymous narrator can tell from George Rouncewell's way of sitting, walking, and brushing his palm across his upper lip, as if there were a great moustache there, that he must "have been a trooper once upon a time."

The reader of *Bleak House* is confronted with a document which he must piece together, scrutinize, interrogate at every turn—in short, interpret—in order to understand. Perhaps the most obvious way in which he is led to do this is the presentation, at the beginning of the novel, of a series of disconnected places and personages—the Court of Chancery, Chesney Wold, Esther Summerson as a child, the Jellyby household and so on. Though the relations among these are withheld from the reader, he assumes that they will turn out to be connected. He makes this assumption according to his acceptance of a figure close to synecdoche, metonymy. Metonymy presupposes a similarity or causality between things presented as contiguous and thereby makes storytelling possible. The reader is encouraged to consider these contiguous items to be in one way or another analo-

gous and to interrogate them for such analogies. Metaphor and metonymy together make up the deep grammatical armature by which
the reader of *Bleak House* is led to make a whole out of discontinuous
parts. At the beginning of the second chapter, for example, when the
narrator shifts "as the crow flies" from the Court of Chancery to
Chesney Wold, he observes that both are alike in being "things of
precedent and usage," and the similarity between Krook and the
Lord Chancellor is affirmed in detail by Krook himself:

> You see I have so many things here . . . of so many kinds,
> and all, as the neighbours think (but *they* know nothing),
> wasting away and going to rack and ruin, that that's why
> they have given me and my place a christening. And I have
> so many old parchmentses and papers in my stock. And I
> have a liking for rust and must and cobwebs. And all's fish
> that comes to my net. And I can't abear to part with any-
> thing I once lay hold of . . . or to alter anything, or to have
> any sweeping, nor scouring, nor cleaning, nor repairing
> going on about me. That's the way I've got the ill name of
> Chancery.

Such passages give the reader hints as to the right way to read
Bleak House. The novel must be understood according to correspondences within the text between one character and another, one scene
and another, one figurative expression and another. If Krook is like
the Lord Chancellor, the various Chancery suitors—Miss Flite,
Gridley, Tom Jarndyce and Richard Carstone—are all alike; there are
similarities between Tulkinghorn, Conversation Kenge and Vholes;
Tom-all-Alone's and Bleak House were both in Chancery; Esther's
doll is duplicated with a difference by the brickmaker's baby, by the
keeper's child at Chesney Wold and by Esther herself. Once the
reader has been alerted to look for such relationships he discovers
that the novel is a complex fabric of recurrences. Characters, scenes,
themes and metaphors return in proliferating resemblances. Each
character serves as an emblem of other similar characters. Each is to
be understood in terms of his reference to others like him. The reader
is invited to perform a constant interpretative dance or lateral movement of cross reference as he makes his way through the text. Each
scene or character shimmers before his eyes as he makes these connections. Think, for example, how many orphans or neglected children there are in *Bleak House,* and how many bad parents. The Lord

Chancellor himself may be included, figuratively, among the latter, since his court was charged in part to administer equity to widows and orphans, those especially unable to take care of themselves. The Chancellor stands *in loco parentis* to Ada and Richard, the "Wards in Chancery."

In this system of reference and counter-reference the differences are, it is important to see, as essential as the similarities. Each lawyer in the novel is different from all the others. Esther did not die, like the brickmaker's baby, though her mother was told that she was dead. The relation between George Rouncewell and his mother is an inverse variant of the theme of bad parents and neglected children. Krook is not the Lord Chancellor. He is only a sign for him. The man himself is kindly enough, though certainly a bit eccentric. The Lord Chancellor is a kindly man too, as he shows in his private interview with Ada and Richard. They are sinister only in their representative capacities, Krook as a symbol of the disorder, avarice and waste of Chancery, the Lord Chancellor as the sign of the authority of his court. An emblem is always to some extent incompatible with its referent. A sign with ominous or deadly meaning may be an innocent enough old weather-beaten board with marks on it when it is seen close up, or it may be the absurd painting of "one impossible Roman upside down," as in the case of the "pointing Allegory" on Mr Tulkinghorn's ceiling. The power of a sign lies not in itself but in what it indicates. *Bleak House* is made up of a multitude of such indications.

Though many of the connections in this elaborate structure of analogies are made explicitly in the text, many are left for the reader to see for himself. One valuable bit of evidence that Dickens took conscious pains to prepare these correspondences is given in his plan for chapter 16. In this chapter Lady Dedlock gets Jo to take her to see the paupers' graveyard where her lover lies buried. Jo points through the iron gate at the spot, and Lady Dedlock asks if it is "consecrated ground." Dickens's notes show that he was aware, and perhaps intended the reader to be aware, of the similarity between Jo's gesture of pointing and the gesture of the pointing Allegory on Mr Tulkinghorn's ceiling. The latter is mentioned in passing earlier in the chapter and of course is made much of at the time of Tulkinghorn's murder. "Jo—," says the note for this chapter, "shadowing forth of Lady Dedlock in the churchyard./Pointing hand of allegory—consecrated ground/'Is it Blessed?' " The two gestures of pointing are

alike, as is suggested by the similarity of pose in the illustrations of
both by "Phiz" for the first editions: "Consecrated ground" and "A
new meaning in the Roman." Both are examples of that procedure of
indication which is the basic structural principle of *Bleak House*. This
procedure is "allegorical" in the strict sense. It speaks of one thing by
speaking of another, as Dickens defines the Court of Chancery by
talking about a rag and bottle shop. Everywhere in *Bleak House* the
reader encounters examples of this technique of "pointing" whereby
one thing stands for another, is a sign for another, indicates another,
can be understood only in terms of another, or named only by the
name of another. The reader must thread his way through the labyrinth of such connections in order to succeed in his interpretation
and solve the mystery of *Bleak House*.

The situation of many characters in the novel is exactly like that
of its writer or reader. So many people in this novel are engaged in
writing or in studying documents, in attempting to decipher what
one chapter-title calls "Signs and Tokens," in learning to read or
write, in hiding documents or in seeking them out, there are so many
references to letters, wills, parchments and scraps of paper, that the
interpretation of signs or of texts may be said to be the fundamental
theme of the novel. Krook's shop is full of old law papers—one of
them, it turns out, perhaps the authentic will for resolving the case of
Jarndyce and Jarndyce. Krook is obsessed, rightly enough, with the
idea that he possesses documents of value, but he does not trust
anyone to read them or to teach him to read. He tries to teach
himself, forming laboriously with chalk on his wall the letters that
spell out "Jarndyce," rubbing out each letter in turn as he makes it.
Miss Flite carries everywhere her reticule full of documents. Richard
broods day and night over the papers in his case, as he is drawn
deeper and deeper into Chancery. Gridley too pores over documents.
Much essential business in this novel, as, to be sure, in many novels,
is carried on by means of letters. Tulkinghorn finds out Lady
Dedlock's secret by the law writing in her lover's hand which matches
the note of instructions Trooper George has from his old officer,
Captain Hawdon. Esther teaches her little maid, Charley, how to
read and write. Mrs Jellyby's irresponsibility is signified in the way
she sits all day writing or dictating letters about Borrioboola-Gha
instead of caring for her family. Poor Caddy Jellyby, her mother's
amanuensis, is bespattered with ink, and Lawyer Tulkinghorn is a

fathomless repository of secrets, all inscribed on the family papers in his strong-boxes.

Some of the most dreamlike and grotesque episodes in the novel involve documents, for example, the chapter in which Grandfather Smallweed, after Krook's death, rummages among the possessions of the deceased, surrounded, in his chair, with great piles of paper, or the chilling scene of the end of Jarndyce and Jarndyce. The latter moves beyond "realism" in the usual sense toward what Baudelaire in "The Essence of Laughter" calls the "dizzy hyperbole" of the "absolute comic":

> It appeared to be something that made the professional gentlemen very merry, for there were several young counsellors in wigs and whiskers on the outside of the crowd, and when one of them told the others about it, they put their hands in their pockets, and quite doubled themselves up with laughter, and went stamping about the pavement of the Hall. . . . [P]resently great bundles of papers began to be carried out—bundles in bags, bundles too large to be got into any bags, immense masses of papers of all shapes and no shapes, which the bearers staggered under, and threw down for the time being, anyhow, on the Hall pavement, while they went back to bring out more. Even these clerks were laughing.

Not to put too fine a point upon it, as Mr Snagsby would say, what is the meaning of all this hermeneutical and archival activity? The reader of the novel must go beyond surface appearances to the deeper coherence of which these surfaces are the dispersed signs. In the same way, many of the characters are cryptographers. They attempt to fit details together to make a pattern revealing some hidden secret. Like Krook they must put "J" and "a" and so on together to spell "Jarndyce." They want to identify the buried truth which is the substance behind the shadowy signs with which they are surrounded, as Richard Carstone believes that there "is—is—must be truth somewhere" "truth and justice" in the case of Jarndyce and Jarndyce. Two motives impel these readers of signs. Like Richard, Gridley or even in spite of herself, Esther, they may want to find out secrets about themselves. Each seeks his unrevealed place in the system of which he is a part. To find out how I am related to others will be to find out who I am, for I am defined by my connections, familial or legal. Esther *is* the illegitimate daughter of Lady Dedlock and Captain Hawdon. Richard *is,* or perhaps is not, a rightful heir to the Jarndyce fortune. Other characters—Mr Tulkinghorn, Guppy, Grandfather Smallweed, Hortense, Mrs Snagsby or Inspector Bucket—want to find out secrets about others. Their motive is the search for power. To find out the hidden place of another in the system is to be able to manipulate him, to dominate him, and of course to make money out of him.

These two versions of the theme of interpretation echo through the novel in melodramatic and parodic forms. Many characters find themselves surrounded by mysterious indications, sinister, threatening or soliciting. Poor Mr Snagsby says, "I find myself wrapped round with secrecy and mystery, till my life is a burden to me." He is "a party to some dangerous secret, without knowing what it is. And it is the fearful peculiarity of this condition that, at any hour of his daily life, . . . the secret may take air and fire, explode, and blow up." Most of the characters are more aggressive than Mr Snagsby in their relation to secrets. Mr Tulkinghorn's "calling is the acquisition of secrets, and the holding possession of such power as they give him, with no sharer or opponent in it." Guppy slowly puts together the evidence of Lady Dedlock's guilt and Esther's parentage. "It's going on," he says of his "case," "and I shall gather it up closer and closer as it goes on." In the same way, Hortense, Lady Dedlock's maid, is "maliciously watchful . . . of everyone and everything," and the "one occupation" of Mrs Snagsby's jealous life "has been . . . to follow Mr Snagsby to and fro, and up and down, and to piece suspicious circumstances together." She has, says Mr Bucket, "done a deal more harm in bringing odds and ends together than if she had meant it." Just as Gridley, Richard, and Miss Flite are obsessed with the documents in their "cases," so the Smallweeds carry on Krook's search for valuable papers after his death, "rummaging and searching, digging, delving, and diving among the treasures of the late lamented." Tom Jarndyce, the original owner of Bleak House, who finally blew out his brains in despair, lived there, "shut up: day and night poring over the wicked heaps of papers in the suit, and hoping against hope to disentangle it from its mystification and bring it to a close." Even Sir Leicester, when he hears the story of a noble lady unfaithful to her husband, "arranges a sequence of events on a plan of his own," and Esther, though she makes no detective effort to uncover the facts about her birth, nevertheless finds Lady Dedlock's face, "in a confused way, like a broken glass to me, in which I saw scraps of old remembrances." She is, in spite of herself, led to put these broken pieces together to mirror the truth about herself, just as, in relation to another secret, she says, "I observed it in many slight particulars, which were nothing in themselves, and only became something when they were pieced together."

The remarkable fact is that these interpreters for the most part are failures. Sometimes their interpretations are false, fictional patterns thrown over the surface of things like a mirage without relation to any deeper truth. Sometimes authentic secrets are discovered but are found out too late or in the wrong way to be of any use to their discoverers. *Bleak House* is full of unsuccessful detectives. The "plan of his own" which Sir Leicester constructs does not save him from the revelation which will shatter his proud complacency. Mrs Snagsby is ludicrously mistaken in her idea that her husband has been unfaithful and is the father of Jo. Krook dies before he finds anything of value in his papers, and even Grandfather Smallweed makes little out of his discovery. Guppy finds out Lady Dedlock's secret, but it does not win him Esther's hand. Gridley dies without resolving his suit. The case of Jarndyce and Jarndyce is used up in costs before the revelation of the newly-discovered will which might have brought it to a close. Even Tulkinghorn and Bucket, the two most clairvoyant and persistent detectives in the novel, are failures. Tulkinghorn is murdered just before he is going to make use of the secret he has discovered about Lady Dedlock. Bucket, in spite of the fact that "the velocity and certainty of [his] interpretation . . . is little short of miraculous," does not save Lady Dedlock. The masterly intuition which leads him to see that she has changed clothes with the brickmaker's wife (another lateral displacement) gets Esther to her mother just too late. They find her "cold and dead" on the steps of Nemo's graveyard. Moreover, the novel is deliberately constructed by Dickens in a way calculated to make the reader a bad detective. Carefully placed clues are designed to lead the reader to believe that either George Rouncewell or Lady Dedlock has murdered Tulkinghorn. Even now, when Dickens's strewing of false clues may seem amateur in comparison with the sophisticated puzzles in modern mystery stories, some readers, one may imagine, are inveigled into thinking that Lady Dedlock is a murderess.

A clue to the meaning of this emphasis on false or fruitless interpretation may be given by what appears to be a fault in the novel. The most salient case of an apparent loose end or inconsistency is the failure to integrate perfectly the two major plots. "[T]he plan, so logical and complete," says Angus Wilson in his recent lively study of Dickens, "by which the Jarndyce lawsuit corrupts all who touch it (save Mr Jarndyce, a nonesuch) is quite upset when we discover that Lady Dedlock's fall from virtue has nothing to do with her being a claimant in the case. The fault is the more glaring because Miss Flite, the little, mad suitor at law, specifically tells how her own sister went to the bad as a result of the misery brought to the family by their legal involvement." This fissure in the novel, a conspicuous rift in its web, seems all the more inexplicable when we consider Dickens's obvious care in other parts of the book to tie together apparently unrelated details. This is done, for example, by the use of a pattern of figurative language which runs throughout the text. One case of this is the apparently trivial metaphor which Dickens uses in the second chapter to describe Lady Dedlock's icy boredom by saying that, unlike Alexander, "having conquered *her* world, [she] fell, not into the melting but rather into the freezing mood." This is picked up in the climactic scenes of her death in the melting snow which lies everywhere and which matches the break in her frigid restraint leading to her death. Surely, the reader supposes, Dickens could have related Lady Dedlock's "crime" more closely to the corrupting effect of Chancery if he had wanted to do so. Perhaps he did not want to. Perhaps he wanted to mislead the reader into thinking that the revelation of Lady Dedlock's secret is at the same time an explanation of the real mystery in the novel—that is, the question of why English society is in such a sad state. At the same time he may have wanted, by leaving the loose end in the open, to invite the reader to investigate further before he takes the revelation of the one mystery as a sufficient explanation of the other. The larger mystery, the mystery of Chancery or of the degeneration of England, is in fact not explained, or if it is explained this is done in so obscure a manner as to leave things at the end of the novel almost as dark, as mud-soaked and fog-drenched, as they are in the opening pages.

The sombre suggestion toward which many elements of the novel lead, like pointers converging from different directions on a single spot, is that the guilty party is not any person or persons, not correctable evil in any institution. The villain is the act of interpretation itself, the naming which assimilates the particular into a system, giving it a definition and a value, incorporating it into a whole.

If this is the case, then in spite of Dickens's generous rage against injustice, selfishness and procrastination, the evil he so brilliantly identifies is irremediable. It is inseparable from language and from the organization of men into society. All proper names, as linguists and ethnologists have recognized, are metaphors. They alienate the person named from his unspeakable individuality and assimilate him into a system of language. They label him in terms of something other than himself, in one form of the differentiating or stepping aside which is the essence of language. To name someone is to alienate him from himself by making him part of a family. Even the orphans or the illegitimate characters in *Bleak House*—Jo, Guster or Esther Summerson—are not free from this alienation. Institutions like Chancery, the workhouse or the Tooting babyfarm where Guster "grew," or persons like Mrs Pardiggle and the Reverend Chadband, act in place of proper parents for such people and force them into social moulds. Everyone in *Bleak House* is, like Jo, made to "move on," in one form or another of the displacement which separates so many of the characters of *Bleak House* from themselves.

It is no accident that the names of so many characters in the novel are either openly metaphorical (Dedlock, Bucket, Guppy, Vholes, Smallweed, Summerson, Badger, Clare, Boythorn, Krook, Swills, Flite, Volumnia) or seem tantalizingly to contain some covert metaphor lying almost on the surface of the word (Tulkinghorn, Turveydrop, Chadband, Pardiggle, Jellyby, Rouncewell, Squod, Bagnet, Snagsby, Skimpole). Each of these names, especially those in the last group, seems to shimmer with multiple meanings drawn from various contexts, like the portmanteau words of "Jabberwocky." They invite etymological interpretation or "explication" in the root sense of an unfolding. Turveydrop? Turf? Turd? Curve? Drop of turf? "Turvey, turvey, clothed in black," as in the children's singing game? An essay could be written exploring the implications of these names. The meaning of names and of naming is, as in Proust's *Remembrance of Things Past,* an important theme in *Bleak House* though Dickens, unlike Proust, seems to remain in that realm of fiction where names truly correspond to the essence of what they name. He does not appear to move on to the stage of disillusion where the incommensurability of name and person or of name and place appears. Dickens's version of this disillusionment, however, is the implicit recognition that the characters to which he gives such emblematic names are linguistic fictions. The metaphors in their names reveal the fact that they are not real people or even copies of real people. They exist only in language. This overt fictionality is Dickens's way of demystifying the belief, affirmed in Plato's *Cratylus,* that the right name gives the essence of the thing. Along with this goes the recognition throughout *Bleak House* that a man's name is a primary way in which he is separated from his privacy and incorporated into society. "Lady Dedlock," says Tulkinghorn in a reproachful reminder of her crime and of her responsibility to the name she has wrongly taken, "here is a family name compromised." Just as Dickens names his characters and helps them do their duty as emblems by borrowing labels for them from other contexts, and just as Miss Flite gives her birds allegorical names which juxtapose the victims of Chancery (Hope, Joy, Youth, and so on), its effects (Dust, Ashes, Waste, Want, Ruin, etc.), and its qualities or the instruments of its deadly fictions (Folly, Words, Wigs, Rags, Sheepskin, Plunder, Precedent, Jargon, Gammon, and Spinach), so the characters have been appropriated by society, named members of it, and cannot escape its coercion.

If the metaphors in the names in *Bleak House* are functional, it is also significant that so many characters have more than one name— nicknames, aliases or occupational names. The effect of these nominal displacements, as the reader shifts from one to another, is to mime in the permutations of language that movement within the social system which prevents each person from being himself and puts him beside himself into some other role. Young Bartholomew Smallweed is "metaphorically called Small and eke Chick Weed, as it were jocularly to express a fledgling." Captain Hawdon takes the alias of "Nemo," "nobody," as if he were trying to escape the involvement in society inevitable if one has any name at all. Gridley is known in the court he haunts as "The man from Shropshire." Tony Jobling takes the alias of Mr Weevle. Jo is called "Toughey" or "The Tough Subject," names pathetically inappropriate. George Rouncewell is "Trooper George." Mr Bagnet is "Lignum Vitae," and Mr Kenge the lawyer has been given the splendid name of "Conversation Kenge." Ada and Richard are "the Wards in Jarndyce," and Miss Flite calls Esther "Fitz-Jarndyce," suggesting thereby not only her relationship to her guardian, John Jarndyce, but also the figurative similarity between her situation as an illegitimate child and the situation of Ada and Richard as wards of the court.

In the context of the sinister connotation of multiple naming in

Bleak House there is something a little disquieting, in spite of its loving intent, in the way Mr Jarndyce gives Esther a multitude of nursery rhyme and legendery pseudonyms, including the name of a fifteenth-century witch: "Old Woman," "Little Old Woman," "Cobweb," "Mrs Shipton," "Mother Hubbard," "Dame Durden." To give someone a nickname is to force on him a metaphorical translation and to appropriate him especially to oneself. This is precisely Jarndyce's selfishness in planning to make Esther his wife, which after all would be another form of renaming. Nor can he protect Esther from her involvement in society by way of her birth. Perhaps her first experience of this is her receipt of a letter from Kenge and Carboy which takes her, as so many characters in the novel are taken, into the legal language which turns her into an object: "We have arrnged for your being forded, carriage free, p^r eight o'clock coach from Reading. . . ." A fit emblem for the violence exercised over the individual by language and other social institutions is that terrifying form of helplessness Esther endures when she lies ill with the smallpox caught from Jo, who caught it from Tom-all-Alone's, the Jarndyce property ruined because it is in Chancery, or perhaps from the place where her unknown father lies buried, "sown in corruption." "Dare I hint," asks Esther, "at that worse time when, strung together somewhere in great black space, there was a flaming necklace, or ring, or starry circle of some kind, of which *I* was one of the beads! And when my only prayer was to be taken off from the rest, and when it was such inexplicable agony and misery to be a part of the dreadful thing!"

Perfect image of the alienation the characters of *Bleak House* suffer by being named members of society! The figure of a moving ring of substitution, in which each person is not himself but part of a system or the sign for some other thing, is used throughout the novel to define those aspects of society Dickens attacks. The evil of Mrs Jellyby's "telescopic philanthropy" or of Mrs Pardiggle's "rapacious benevolence" is that they treat people not as individuals but as elements in a system of abstract do-gooding. Mrs Pardiggle has "a mechanical way of taking possession of people," "a show . . . of doing charity by wholesale, and of dealing in it to a large extent," and a voice "much too business-like and systematic." The world of aristocratic fashion is a "brilliant and distinguished circle," "tremendous orb, nearly five miles round," just as London as a whole is a "great tee-totum . . . set up for its daily spin and whirl." Within her circle Lady Dedlock lives imprisoned "in the desolation of Boredom and the clutch of Giant Despair": substituting one place for another in a perpetually unsuccessful attempt to escape from her consciousness of the false self she has assumed. "Weariness of soul lies before her, as it lies behind . . . but the imperfect remedy is always to fly, from the last place where it has been experienced."

A similar metaphor is used in the satire of representative government. It underlies that brilliant chapter in which the ruling classes gather at Chesney Wold to discuss the dissolution of Parliament and the formation of a new Government. (John Butt and Kathleen Tillotson in the article cited above discuss the references here to Disraeli, Russell, and the Parliamentary crises of the early fifties.) Representative government is another form of delegation. Each Member of Parliament acts as the synecdochic sign for his constituents. Dickens, as is well known, had little faith in this form of government. The relation between representative and represented is always indirect. Any authentic correspondence between sign and signified is lost in the process of mediation. When Sir Thomas Doodle undertakes to form a new ministry he "throw[s] himself upon the country," but this throwing is only figurative, "chiefly in the form of sovereigns and beer." This has the advantage over direct appeal to the voters that "in this metamorphosed state he is available in a good many places simultaneously, and can throw himself upon a considerable portion of the country at one time." In the practice of parliamentary government the People are no more than "a certain large number of supernumeraries, who are to be occasionally addressed, and relied upon for shouts and choruses, as on the theatrical stage." The actual business of governing is carried on by a small group of leaders of the two parties, Lord Coodle, Sir Thomas Doodle and so on down to Poodle and Quoodle on one side, Buffy, Cuffy, Duffy, Fuffy, Guffy and so on on the other. The comic names admirably suggest not only the anonymity of these men but the fact that each may replace any of the others. They exist, like the letters of the alphabet which Krook or Charlie Neckett so painfully learn, as the possibility of an inexhaustible set of permutations and combinations in which Noodle would replace Moodle; Puffy, Muffy; Puffy, Poodle; or Nuffy, Noodle, and nothing would be changed at all. Government is a circular game of substitutions like the nursery rhyme based on the letters of the alphabet beginning "A was an apple-pie."

This nursery rhyme, incorporated into another reference to the basic elements of language and to naming as the absorption of the particular into a system, is referred to in John Jarndyce's analysis of the Court of Chancery. Chancery, he says, is a dance or round. It proceeds through interminable linguistic substitutions replacing one declaration by another and never getting closer to any end. People, once they are named parties to a suit, are swept into the ring, as Esther is caught in her dream necklace, and can never hope to escape. No other text identifies so well the structure of *Bleak House* as a work of literature and also the structure of the society it describes. "It's about a Will, and the trusts under a Will—or it was, once," says Jarndyce.

> It's about nothing but Costs, now. We are always appear-
> ing, and disappearing, and swearing, and interrogating,
> and filing, and cross-filing, and arguing, and sealing, and
> motioning, and referring, and reporting, and revolving
> about the Lord Chancellor and all his satellites, and equi-
> tably waltzing ourselves off to dusty death, about
> Costs. . . . Law finds it can't do this, Equity finds it can't
> do that; neither can so much as say it can't do anything,
> without this solicitor instructing and this counsel appear-
> ing for A, and that solicitor instructing and that counsel
> appearing for B; and so on through the whole alphabet,
> like the history of the Apple Pie. And thus, through years
> and years, and lives and lives, everything goes on, con-
> stantly beginning over and over again, and nothing ever
> ends. And we can't get out of the suit on any terms, for we
> are made parties to it, and *must be* parties to it, whether we
> like it or not.

"Nothing ever ends"—an important thematic stand of the novel is the special mode of temporal existence in an unjust society, or perhaps under any social order. Such an order has replaced realities by signs, substances by shadows. Each sign, in such a "system," refers not to a reality but to another sign which precedes it and which is pure anteriority in the sense that it refers back in its turn to another sign. A sign by definition designates what is absent, something which may exist but which at present is not here, as the cross on the top of St Paul's Cathedral, "so golden, so high up, so far out of his reach," is a "sacred emblem" indicating the apparent absence of God from Jo's life. A sign which refers back to another sign designates what is in its turn another absence. Gridley, the "Man from Shropshire," protests against the explanation of his suffering which blames it all on that code of equity which Conversation Kenge calls "a very great system, a very great system." "There again!" says Gridley. "The system! I am told, on all hands, it's the system. I mustn't look to individuals. It's the system. I mustn't go into Court, and say, "My Lord, I beg to know this from you—is this right or wrong? Have you the face to tell me I have received justice, and therefore am dismissed? My Lord knows nothing of it. He sits there, to administer the system.""

In spite of Dickens's sympathy for Gridley's indignant outrage, the whole bent of *Bleak House* is toward indicating that it is in fact the systematic quality of organized society which causes Gridley's suffering—not a bad system of law, but any system, not a bad representative government, but the institution itself, not the special evil of aristocratic family pride, but any social organization based on membership in a family. As soon as a man becomes in one way or another part of such a system, born into it or made a party to it, he enters into a strange kind of time. He loses any possibility of ever having a present self or a present satisfaction, loses any possibility of ever going back to find the origin of his present plight, loses the possibility of ever escaping from his present restless state or of making any end to it other than "dusty death." This intolerable experience of time is dramatized with admirable explicitness, not only in the Chancery suit which can never end except in its consumption in costs, but also in the unhappy life of Richard Carstone. If no proper "Will" or explicable origin of Jarndyce and Jarndyce can ever be found (there are in fact three wills in the case), Richard as a result lives in perpetual deferring or postponement, never able to settle down to a profession or to commit himself to a present project. He dwells in a continual expectation of a settlement which can never come: "Everything postponed to that imaginary time! Everything held in confusion and indecision until then!" "The uncertainties and delays of the Chancery suit" have made him unlike his natural self and have "imparted to his nature something of the careless spirit of a gamester, who [feels] that he [is] part of a great gaming system." "Now?" asks Richard. "There's no now for us suitors." If there is no now there is also no past or future for people who have been forced to accept their membership in a pattern of signs without substance. Each element in such a game refers to other elements in it, in a perpetually frustrated movement which can hope for no end. The other nightmare of Esther's dream expresses this perfectly: "I laboured up colossal staircases, ever striving to reach the top, and ever turned, as I have seen a worm in a garden path, by some obstruction, and labouring again."

Miss Flite, mad as she is, is close to the truth about Chancery when she says, "I expect a Judgment. On the day of Judgment. And shall then confer estates." The only escape from the circle of signs would be the end of the world or death, that "beginning the world" which Richard undertakes at the moment he dies, but "Not this world, O not this! The world that sets this right." Dickens here, as in his work throughout, suggests an absolute incompatibility between this world and the far-off supernatural world. The many deaths in *Bleak House* have a significance somewhat different from that in many novels. In fiction generally, according to Walter Benjamin, the reader enjoys vicariously a finality he can never experience directly in his own life, my death being on principle an end I shall never be able to view in retrospect. In a novel, says Benjamin, the "meaning" of each character's life "is revealed only in his death," and "what draws the reader to the novel is the hope of warming his shivering life with a death he reads about." Certainly there are in *Bleak House* many deaths to read about. Their peculiarity is that they are not satisfactory ends for the lives of those who die. Each character who dies passes suddenly from one world to another, leaving his affairs in this world as unsettled and as unfinished as ever. Krook dies without discovering the secrets in his papers. Gridley dies without resolving his suit, as Richard is killed by the final frustration of his hopes for an end to his case. Tulkinghorn dies without being able to use the power he has gained over Lady Dedlock. Jo's death is elaborately portrayed as the final example of his "moving on." The deaths of *Bleak House* constitute only in a paradoxical way "ends" which establish the destinies of those who die. Their deaths define them once and for all as people whose lives were unfinished, as people who never achieved the peace of a settlement. Their lives had meaning only in reference to the perpetually unsettled system of which they were part.

Bleak House itself has exactly the same structure as the society it exposes. It too assimilates everything it touches into a system of meaning. In the novel each phrase is alienated from itself and made into a sign of some other phrase. If the case of Jarndyce and Jarndyce is a "masterly fiction," and if many characters in the novel spend their time reading or writing, *Bleak House* is a masterly fiction too, and Dickens too spent his time, like Mrs Jellyby, covering paper with ink, his eye fixed not on his immediate surroundings but on an imaginary world. The novel too has a temporal structure without proper origin, present or end. It too is made up of an incessant movement of reference in which each element leads to other elements in a constant displacement of meaning. *Bleak House* is properly allegorical, according to a definition of allegory as a temporal system of cross references among signs rather than as a spatial pattern of correspondence between signs and referents. Most people in the novel live without understanding their plight. The novel, on the other hand, gives the reader the information necessary to understand why the characters suffer, and at the same time the power to understand that the novel is fiction rather than mimesis. The novel calls attention to its own procedures and confesses to its own rhetoric, not only, for example, in the onomastic system of metaphorical names already discussed, but also in the insistent metaphors of the style throughout.

Each character in *Bleak House* is not only named in metaphor but speaks according to his own private system of metaphors. Moreover, he is spoken of by the narrators in metaphors which recur. Nor are these metaphors allowed to remain "buried." In one way or another they are brought into the open. Their figurative quality is insisted upon. In this way the reader has constantly before him one version of the interpretative act whereby nothing is separately itself, but can be named only in its relation to some other thing. Dickens is master of an artificial style which makes its artifice obvious. Among the innumerable examples of this, the following contains the linguistic texture of the novel in miniature: "The Mercuries, exhausted by looking out of window, are reposing in the hall; and hang their heavy heads, the gorgeous creatures, like overblown sun-flowers. Like them too, they seem to run to a deal of seed in their tags and trimmings." The nominal metaphor (Mercuries) has been used throughout to label the Dedlock footmen. To this is here added a second figure, a metaphor of a metaphor. These Mercuries are like gorgeous sunflowers. To name them in this way has a double effect. It invites the reader to think of real footmen being described by the narrator in ornately witty language. This language names them as something other than themselves, but it also calls attention to its own wit, uncovers it by playing with it and extending it. The reader knows it is "just a figure of speech." The footmen are not Mercuries, nor are they sunflowers. These are ways of talking about them which bring them vividly before the reader and express the narrator's ironic scorn for aristocratic display. At the same time, the figures and figures within figures remind the reader that there are no real footmen in the novel. The Mercuries have only a linguistic existence. They exist as metaphors, and the reader can reach them only through Dickens's figurative language. This is true for all the characters and events in the novel. The fabric of Dickens's style is woven of words in which each takes its meaning not from something outside words, but from other words. The footmen are to be understood only in terms of Mercury, Mercury only in terms of sunflowers. This way of establishing a fictional reality matches the kind of existence the characters in the novel have. They too are helpless parts of a structure based on words.

Does the novel propose any escape from this situation, or is it a wholly negative work? How might one step outside the ring? Esther Summerson and John Jarndyce are the chief examples in *Bleak House* of Dickens's commitment to a Christian humanism compounded of belief in "the natural feelings of the heart," in unselfish engagement in duty and industrious work, in spontaneous charity toward those immediately within one's circle, and of faith that Providence secretly governs all in this lower world. This Providence will reward the good with another existence not cursed by the shadow of indefinite postponement. John Jarndyce has "resolutely kept himself outside the circle" of Chancery, holding himself free of its false hopes in an heroic effort of detachment. "Trust in nothing but in Providence and your own efforts," he tells Richard. He uses his apparently inexhaustible money to do good quietly to those around him, loving all, asking nothing in return, and purging himself ultimately from his one selfishness, the desire to take Esther as his wife. He is Dickens's most successful version of that recurrent personage in his fiction, the benevolent-father figure.

Esther has been much maligned by critics for her coy revelations of how good she is, how much she is loved, and for her incorrigible habit of crying for joy. Nevertheless, she is in fact a plausible characterization, more palatable perhaps if one recognizes the degree to which the other narrator is an ironic commentary on her language, her personality, and her way of seeing things. She has reacted to the harsh teaching of her godmother's "distorted religion" ("It would have been far better, little Esther, that you had had no birthday; that you had never been born!" by resolving "to be industrious, contented and kind-hearted, and to do some good to some one, and win some love to myself." The emotional logic of this reaction is well known by now, and it is acutely rendered by Dickens, though we would perhaps be less inclined than he to admire its indirections. As opposed to Mrs Pardiggle's abstract and wholesale philanthropy, Esther thinks it best "to be as useful as I [can], and to render what kind services I [can], to those immediately about me." She is conspicuously unwilling to engage in that form of the will to power which infects so many others in the book, the desire to decipher signs and to ferret out secrets. "Duty, duty, Esther" is her motto. She strikes out "a natural, wholesome, loving course of industry and perseverance," ringing herself into her household tasks with a merry little peal of her bundle of keys. These are the symbols of her power to "sweep the cobwebs out of the sky," like the little old woman in the nursery rhyme, and to bring order everywhere she goes.

Even so, the interpretation of Jarndyce and Esther cannot be so straightforward. Perplexing puzzles and inconsistencies remain. What *is* the source of Jarndyce's money? It must come by inheritance and through his membership in the Jarndyce family, since he is never shown lifting a finger to earn any of it. This kind of inheritance, however, is shown throughout the novel to involve a man, in spite of himself, in the evils of "system." Moreover, there are many ways to exercise power over others. Not the least effective of these is self-abnegation. There is a kind of coercion in Jarndyce's goodness. He gives Esther to Allan Woodcourt without consulting her in the matter, and there is something a little unsettling about the fact that the new Bleak House, exact duplicate of the old, built secretly by Jarndyce for Esther and Allan, is another example of that theme of doubling which has such dark implications elsewhere in the novel. The patterns created by the lives of the good characters correspond rigorously to the patterns in the lives of the bad. This is as true for Esther as for Jarndyce. If Chancery is a "system" which sweeps everything it encounters into its dance, Esther, in another disquieting detail, is said by Harold Skimpole to be "intent upon the perfect working of the whole little orderly system of which [she is] the centre." If old Mr Turveydrop's falseness is expressed by the fact that he forms himself after the Prince Regent and is a "Model of Deportment," Bucket praises Esther's courage when they are tracking down her mother by saying, "You're a pattern, you know, that's what you are, . . . you're a pattern."

Bleak House is a powerful book, an extraordinary work of Dickens's creative power. It is also to some degree a painful book. The pain lies partly in its prevailing darkness or bleakness, its presentation of so many admirably comic creations who are at the same time distorted, grotesque, twisted (Krook, Grandfather Smallweed, Mrs Jellyby, Chadband, Guppy, Miss Flite—what a crew!). It is painful also because of its self-contradictions. Like the case of Jarndyce and Jarndyce it remains unfinished at its end, a tissue of loose ends and questions rather than of neatly resolved patterns. As in all Dickens's work, there is at the centre of *Bleak House* a tension between belief in some extra-human source of value, a stable centre outside the shadows of the human game, and on the other hand the shade of a suspicion that there may be no such centre, that all systems of interpretation may be fictions.

In *Bleak House* this tension is dramatized in a way appropriate for a novel which focuses on the theme of interpretation. It lies in the contrast between Esther's way of seeing the world and that of the anonymous narrator. Skimpole, Chadband, Mrs Jellyby and the rest each dwell hermetically sealed within an idiosyncratic system of language. In particular, Skimpole's light-hearted reading of the world as designed for his delectation and amusement, expressed with great verve by Dickens, is a frighteningly plausible reversal of Esther's commitment to duty and responsibility. Esther's language too is a special perspective, perhaps a distorting one, as is the view of the other narrator. Each has his characteristic rhetoric, a rhetoric which interprets the world along certain lines. To Esther the course of her life seems secretly governed by a divine Providence. She sees this most concretely in the benign presences she glimpses in the landscape around Chesney Wold: "O, the solemn woods over which the light and shadow travelled swiftly, as if Heavenly wings were sweeping on benignant errands through the summer air." To the other narrator no such presences are visible. He sees a world darkening toward death, a world in which it is always foggy or raining. His vision, for example in the description of Tom-all-Alone's in chapter 46, may be defined as nihilistic: "Darkness rests upon Tom-all-Alone's. Dilating and dilating since the sun went down last night, it has gradually swelled until it fills every void in the place. . . . The blackest nightmare in the infernal stables grazes on Tom-all-Alone's, and Tom is fast asleep." Which of these is a misinterpretation? Perhaps both are? Though the happy ending of *Bleak House* may beguile the reader into accepting Esther's view as the true one, the novel does not resolve the incompatibility between her vision and what the other narrator sees. The meaning of the novel lies in this irresolution.

Like many other nineteenth-century writers Dickens was caught between his desire to reject what he found morally objectionable or false about Christianity, in particular its doctrine of original sin, and his desire to retain some form of Christian morality. This retention was for Dickens, as for others in his time, the only protection against nihilism. *Bleak House* presents the reader with a sick, decaying, moribund society. It locates with profound insight the causes of that sickness in the sign-making power, in the ineradicable human tendency to take the sign for the substance, and in the instinctive habit of interpretation, assimilating others into a private or collective system of meaning. At the same time the novel itself performs a large-scale act of interpretation. If there were no interpretation there would be no novel. It frees itself from the guilt of this only by giving the reader, not least in its inconsistencies, the evidence necessary to see that it *is* an interpretation.

On the one hand the distorted Christianity of Esther's aunt is firmly repudiated. Against her, "Watch ye therefore! lest coming suddenly he find you sleeping," is set Jesus's forgiveness of the woman caught in adultery: "He that is without sin among you, let him first cast a stone at her!" On the other hand, the novel apparently sustains Lady Dedlock in her remorse, in her somewhat narrowly Christian interpretation of what from another point of view, abundantly suggested in the novel, is her natural and good love for Captain Hawdon. A later generation might see marriage as one of the perfidious legalities distorting the natural feelings of the heart. In fact in Dickens's own day Ludwig Feuerbach in *The Essence of Christianity,* George Eliot in her liaison with George Henry Lewes, perhaps even in her fiction, and Anthony Trollope in such a novel as *Dr Wortle's School* saw individual acts of love as sanctifying the legal institution of marriage rather than the other way around. Lady Dedlock's mystery and the mystery of Chancery are so closely intertwined that the reader may be enticed into thinking that the solution of the one is the solution of the other. Some "illicit" act like fornication must lie at the origin of Jarndyce and Jarndyce and be the explanation of the suffering it causes, visiting the sins of the fathers on the children, generation after generation. The novel persuasively shows, however, that nothing lies at the origin of Jarndyce and Jarndyce but man's ability to create and administer systems of law. Such systems give actions and documents a meaning. It would seem, nevertheless, that the Ten Commandments fit this definition of evil as well as the laws and precedents governing Chancery. Both the particular commandments against which Lady Dedlock has sinned and the system of Chancery have jurisdiction over the relations of man to woman, parent to child. Between its commitment to a traditional interpretation of these relations and a tendency to put all interpretation in question as the original evil *Bleak House* remains poised.

Esther Summerson Rehabilitated

Alex Zwerdling

The critics have not been kind to Esther Summerson. From the first, her prominence in *Bleak House* has been treated as one of Dickens's disastrous mistakes. George Henry Lewes was not the last critic to consider her a "monstrous failure." The portrait of Esther is said to be unrealistic and unconvincing, since a girl with so little experience of the world could hardly be expected to understand the complex institutions and devious characters she is asked to describe. It is regularly assumed that Dickens tires of the "mask" of Esther and uses her as a mouthpiece at will, a practice that would certainly create a hopelessly inconsistent character. Esther is also frequently accused of coyness, particularly in her insistence on disclaiming the compliments heaped upon her while faithfully recording them. In the sarcastic words of the original review in the *Spectator:* "It is impossible to doubt the simplicity of her nature, because she never omits to assert it with emphasis."

These attitudes seem to me based on a serious misunderstanding of Esther Summerson and of Dickens's purpose in making her so prominent in *Bleak House*. She is, I think, one of the triumphs of his art, a subtle psychological portrait clear in its outlines and convincing in its details. But in order to understand what Dickens was doing, we must rid ourselves of certain critical clichés: that he was not interested in point of view, that his characters are static and shallow, and that his psychological penetration was not remarkable. In calling

From *PMLA* 88, no. 3 (May 1973). © 1973 by the Modern Language Association of America.

these attitudes critical clichés, I am not ignoring a number of studies which have treated Dickens's interest in psychology more positively, but suggesting that this new perspective has still not become dominant.

An accurate assessment of Dickens's portrait of Esther must, I think, begin with his interest in first-person narratives. In *David Copperfield, Bleak House,* and *Great Expectations* he used this technical device to record in depth a long process of psychological development. Dickens's (and the reader's) attitude toward these narrators is seldom straightforward. Our perspective must be detached and critical, since we are intended to see more than the narrator sees. In all three novels, Dickens further makes use of a double perspective even in the narrator by shifting back and forth from his childish to his adult vision. This temporal double perspective is much more consistently used in *David Copperfield* and *Great Expectations* than in *Bleak House,* however, because in that novel Dickens is interested in portraying someone who remains trapped between childhood and real maturity. Such a narrator is not a transparent medium for the author's impressions. We are asked to look very much *at* Esther rather than *through* her, to observe her actions, her fantasies, even her verbal mannerisms with great attention. For Dickens's attitude toward her is essentially clinical, and the major aim of her portion of the narrative is to study in detail the short- and long-range effect of a certain kind of adult violence on the mind of a child.

"The crime against the child," as Dorothy Van Ghent has suggested, is one of Dickens's major themes. Between *Oliver Twist* and *Bleak House,* his vision of childhood suffering became much more psychological. Oliver's deprivation is primarily physical, external. By the time Dickens came to write *Dombey and Son,* he had become more interested in the child deprived of love than of food and shelter, and this shift is clearly reflected both in *David Copperfield* and in *Bleak House.* Esther's first memories of her aunt (the "godmother" who brought her up) obliquely record both the withholding of love and the overwhelming sense of failure it imprints on the child:

> I was brought up, from my earliest remembrance—like some of the princesses in the fairy stories, only I was not charming—by my godmother. . . . She was handsome; and if she had ever smiled, would have been (I used to think) like an angel—but she never smiled. . . . I felt so

different from her, even making every allowance for the differences between a child and a woman; I felt so poor, so trifling, and so far off; that I never could be unrestrained with her—no, could never even love her as I wished. It made me very sorry to consider how good she was, and how unworthy of her I was; and I used ardently to hope that I might have a better heart; and I talked it over very often with the dear old doll; but I never loved my god-mother as I ought to have loved her, and as I felt I must have loved her if I had been a better girl.

There is very little independent judgment in this passage, hardly any sense of a code that would justify the child and condemn the god-mother, although of course Dickens relies on the reader to supply such a perspective on Esther's words. Rather, Esther seems to have accepted the values by which she is found "poor" and "trifling." All the guilt and shame are taken upon herself. Such self-denigration becomes Esther's essential life-style. Deprived of the sense of her own merit from earliest infancy, she is never sure that she is worthy of love and respect. The innumerable compliments on her wisdom, shrewdness, affectionate nature, and beauty she compulsively records and compulsively dismisses as absurd. She has an insatiable hunger for them, yet they are never the right food, for the damage to her sense of self-esteem has been permanent. This complex behavior is what critics of the novel have usually called her "coyness."

It is appropriate, rather, to use the word trauma, to see Esther's childhood as a wound that never fully heals. The traumatic experience in the narrow sense of the term is the scene in which her illegitimacy is revealed, when on her birthday she asks her godmother about her parentage. The stern reply etches itself on her mind in precise detail and is never forgotten:

> Your mother, Esther, is your disgrace, and you were hers. The time will come—and soon enough—when you will understand this better, and will feel it too, as no one save a woman can. . . . Submission, self-denial, diligent work, are the preparations for a life begun with such a shadow on it. You are different from other children, Esther, because you were not born, like them, in common sinfulness and wrath. You are set apart.
>
> (chap. 3)

I hope to show that Esther's reaction to this speech can be understood along the lines of Erik Erikson's description of trauma: "an experience characterized by impressions so sudden, or so powerful, or strange that they cannot be assimilated at the time and, therefore, persist from stage to stage as a foreign body seeking outlet or absorption and imposing on all development a certain irritation causing stereotypy and repetitiveness" (*Gandhi's Truth: On the Origin of Militant Nonviolence*). Years later, on two subsequent occasions, Esther accurately recalls portions of this speech (chaps. 17, 36). Her godmother's words (and the coldness of heart behind them) become the most powerful determinant of her adult personality and life choices. This has often been recognized; what has not so generally been understood is that Dickens creates, in Esther's narrative, a detailed life pattern that records both the long-range effects of this childhood trauma and the stages of an attempt to triumph over it.

Esther is wounded by her godmother's speech but she is not crushed. She has a supremely practical turn of mind, and her first impulse is to formulate a strategy for survival. "Submission, self-denial, diligent work" is what her godmother proposes. Esther's own plan is a subtle but significant variant: "I would try, as hard as ever I could, to repair the fault I had been born with (of which I confessedly felt guilty and yet innocent), and would strive as I grew up to be industrious, contented, and kind-hearted, and to do some good to some one, and win some love to myself if I could" (chap. 3). An instinct for self-preservation is at work in this formula. Although she has been told to feel only guilt, she also feels a paradoxical innocence. And the grim words "submission, self-denial, diligent work" are transformed into more social and less self-destructive terms: contentment, kindheartedness, industry. Above all, Esther sees even those devices as means to an end: to "win some love to myself if I could." It is as if the child instinctively understands this basic psychological necessity and determines to direct all its energies toward obtaining it.

Esther envisages love as a reward for strenuous effort, however, not as something that may come naturally; and she does not specify what *kind* of love she is talking about. It would, of course, be absurd to expect a child to distinguish among the various kinds of love, parental, romantic, conjugal, filial, and so on. But in fact the ambiguity of the phrase illuminates Esther's most important adult conflicts. As we gradually begin to understand, she has great doubts about her right to love and marry, and she accepts with misgiving the role of an affectionate spectator of other people's attachments. There is a buried but potent feeling that the "sin" of being illegitimate makes her unfit for romantic love.

Others conspire to make Esther see herself in this light. It is curious, for example, that she is never for a moment considered a possible match for Richard, that she is instantly cast in the role of duenna in his romance with Ada. Richard meets the two girls at the same time. They are approximately the same age, both attractive, and both attracted to him. Yet from the first Jarndyce takes Esther into his confidence concerning his hopes for the union of the other two. Esther's reaction to this arrangement is complex, though she does her best to make it simple: "My fancy, made a little wild by the wind perhaps, would not consent to be all unselfish, either, though I would have persuaded it to be so if I could. It wandered back to my godmother's house, and came along the intervening track, raising up shadowy speculations which had sometimes trembled there in the dark, as to what knowledge Mr. Jarndyce had of my earliest history" (chap. 6). Such ungrateful and dangerous speculations must be suppressed; indeed, they can hardly be recorded without guilt, even in the deliberately obscure and general terms Esther uses. She instantly calls her errant "fancy" back to duty: "It was not for me to muse over bygones, but to act with a cheerful spirit and a grace-ful heart. So I said to myself, 'Esther, Esther, Esther! Duty, my dear!' " (chap. 6).

In this impatient command, Esther temporarily resigns her own hopes of romance and begins to live vicariously in the love of Richard and Ada. She cannot treat the idea of having a lover as a serious possibility or as her right. She begins to think of herself as (and allows people to treat her as) "a methodical, old-maidish sort of foolish little person" (chap. 8). She offers no objection to being called a whole string of pet names—"Old Woman, and Little Old Woman, and Cobweb, and Mrs. Shipton, and Mother Hubbard, and Dame Durden, and so many names of that sort, that my own name soon became quite lost among them" (chap. 8). These names have a double function: they substitute the image of an old, maternal, drudging woman for the image of a young girl; and they suggest that the only fit mate for such a person is an aging, paternal man like Mr. Jarndyce.

Her buried romantic impulse is almost entirely invested in her vicarious participation in the Ada-Richard courtship. She is the Nurse in the lovers' acting out of *Romeo and Juliet,* and her fantasies are obviously filled with displaced romance: "They brought a chair on either side of me, and put me between them, and really seemed to have fallen in love with me, instead of one another" (chap. 13). When the marriage finally takes place, there is very little romance left. Richard is nearly penniless and driven half-wild by the Chancery suit; Ada marries him in secret against her guardian's wishes. When Esther realizes that their marriage will exclude her, as all marriages must, she is driven wild with grief: "I walked up and down in a dim corner, sobbing and crying" (chap. 51). On the same evening, she steals back to their house and stands by their door, listening for "the murmur of their young voices" (chap. 51). After the courtship, the duenna must turn voyeur.

The strangest aspect of Esther's relationship to the lovers is her attitude toward Ada. Her intense attachment is irrational and mysterious and no commonsense explanation of it will serve. In part, Esther's adoration of Ada is a displaced form of romantic love, inhibited from expressing itself normally by her fear that she is forbidden to marry. But she has also from the first treated Ada as an idealized second self, as the girl she might have become if she had not been born "different from other children" and "set apart." Her fantasy-identification with Ada makes it possible for Esther to bear a great deal of humiliation and deprivation. It is as though she lived in the belief that no evil could affect her alter ego, no matter what happened to herself. When she realizes she is ill, she commands her maid to bar the door to Ada: "Charley, if you let her in but once, only to look upon me for one moment as I lie here, I shall die" (chap. 31). Not "she will die," but "I shall die." Her need to protect Ada is an oblique form of self-preservation. When, after her disfigurement, she calls Ada "my beauty," as she frequently does, the phrase is charged with meaning.

We are dealing here with one set of consequences arising from Esther's childhood wound, her surrender of the normal expectation of love and marriage and the attempt to feed her need for romance vicariously. These are not the only long-range consequences of her unsponsored childhood: there is also the inhibition of her natural intelligence. She has been made to feel inferior to others in every way. What then is she to make of the fact that her natural intelligence and her power of observation are unusually acute? She consistently tries to deny her abilities, as in her first words to the reader: "I have a great deal of difficulty in beginning to write my portion of these pages, for I know I am not clever. I always knew that. . . . I had always rather a noticing way—not a quick way, O no!—a silent way of noticing what passed before me, and thinking I should like to understand it better. I have not by any means a quick understanding. When I love a person very tenderly indeed, it seems to brighten. But even that may be my vanity" (chap. 3). The reflex quality of the disclaimers in this passage ("not a quick way, O no!" "But even that may be my vanity") suggests how efficiently she has been bullied into denying any sense of her own worth. Vanity and pride are her great fears; she has never been taught a comparable fear of underestimating herself.

Esther does indeed have "rather a noticing way," a sharp analytic intelligence and a keen sense of the disparity between peoples' words and their actions. Yet her observant satirical eye is regularly reproved by her conformist conscience. Here she is, for example, on Mrs. Badger:

also see Harold Skimpole P. 46

> She was surrounded in the drawing-room by various objects, indicative of her painting a little, playing the piano a little, playing the guitar a little, playing the harp a little, singing a little, working a little, reading a little, writing poetry a little, and botanising a little. . . . If I add, to the little list of her accomplishments, that she rouged a little, I do not mean that there was any harm in it.
>
> (chap. 13)

If Dickens were describing Mrs. Badger in his own voice, only the last phrase would be out of place. It would have to be made obviously (rather than ambiguously) ironic or else eliminated altogether. But for Esther to draw in her claws and play the kitten in this way is essential to her image of herself. Her critical sense is often disguised as mere reportorial accuracy. When its satiric content becomes too dangerous, it is suddenly replaced by a fraudulent generosity of spirit. It is no wonder that critics are confused about Esther's intelligence and tempted by the theory that she becomes, at moments, merely Dickens's mouthpiece. But the difference between Dickens and Esther as narrators lies not in their perceptiveness but in their self-confidence *about* their perceptiveness. The savage sarcasm of the other narrator of *Bleak House* is simply a psychological impossibility for Esther.

It should be clear from these illustrations that Dickens's interest in Esther is fundamentally clinical: to observe and describe a certain kind of psychic debility. The psychological subject matter of Dickens's later novels demanded a new narrative technique, in which the character could present himself directly, rather than being described and interpreted by an omniscient narrator. Esther Summerson is Dickens's most ambitious attempt to allow a character who does not fully understand herself to tell her own story. There are obvious dangers in such a technique. The reader may not be able to see beyond the narrator's vision, although he needs to do so if he is to comprehend the book. Furthermore, a neurotic character will be obsessive, and the narrative will inevitably keep recording his obsessions, often at the price of variety. Certainly *Bleak House* does not escape these dangers. Yet the portrait would be less subtle, detailed, and vivid if it were not done in the first person. Esther's story must be told from the inside; and if we are to feel that the damage to her psyche has in some sense been permanent, it cannot be told by a fully mature woman looking back on the troubles of her youth.

There are important thematic, situational, and psychological parallels between Esther's case and those of other people in the novel. In allowing her to tell her own story, Dickens gives selflessness a voice and tries to provide words for some of society's usually inarticulate victims. She is the unconscious representative of the many characters in *Bleak House* who have not known parental love—Jo, the Jellybys, the Pardiggles, Guster, Prince Turveydrop, Richard, Ada. The breakdown of the parent-child relationship is one of the major themes of the novel. Parents behave like children; children must take over parental roles. The Lord High Chancellor "appeared so poor a substitute for the love and pride of parents" (chap. 3). And the universe, as Mr. Jarndyce points out sadly, "makes rather an indifferent parent" (chap. 6). Yet all the other victims of this parentless world are seen from the outside. We are conscious of their numbers and of their superficial trials, but we know little of the internal cost of this absence of nurture. The function of Esther's narrative, then, is to show us the deeper and more lasting effects of such neglect.

Esther is also the representative of another inarticulate character in *Bleak House*—Lady Dedlock, whose *inner* history Dickens could not write for a Victorian audience. The two women seem totally different yet are in a similar position. Each is alienated from her true self and unable to acknowledge her deepest feelings. Each is incomplete: Lady Dedlock searches for a child; Esther for a mother. Lady

Dedlock has given up her lover and married an affectionate and protecting man a generation older than herself, whom she respects but does not love—the very doom that Esther narrowly escapes. The mother's haughtiness and isolation are as much aspects of a frustrating role as the daughter's cheerfulness and immersion in the community. The two women specialize in opposing parts of themselves rather than allowing their complex natures full play.

The final reason that Esther must tell her own story is connected with Dickens's attitude toward the qualities she embodies. Whether that attitude is at all ironic has always been one of the major problems in interpreting the book. First-person narratives frequently produce such disagreements, and for understandable reasons, since it is impossible for the author to comment directly on the character he has created. Yet this deliberate surrender of the power of judgment can be useful to a writer whose response to a particular way of life is fundamentally divided. Its poetic equivalent—the dramatic monologue—has frequently been used in the same way. Both make it possible for a writer whose feelings about a character are simultaneously sympathetic and hostile to write about him without self-contradiction. Esther Summerson's narrative may finally be a way for Dickens to study the psychological roots of selflessness, a trait about which his feelings were profoundly ambiguous, without committing himself to either praise or blame.

II

I have suggested that Esther is not a static character, and that Dickens is interested in tracing various patterns of behavior in her from infancy to adulthood. In becoming the ward of Mr. Jarndyce, Esther is given a chance to relive her childhood with a radically different parental figure, generous, loving, and open. Consequently she acquires two entirely different images of herself, the rejected and the sponsored child, and these two identities engage in a long civil war for control of her psyche. It is the task of her early adult years to absorb the new image and permit it to affect every aspect of her life, her sense of her own abilities and rights, her assessment of other people, and her life plans. Dickens has a remarkable feeling for the difficulty of this task and understands how potent the curse of childhood deprivation can be, no matter what may happen in later life.

The first signs of a new self-appraisal are seen in Esther's judgment of other people, which becomes steadily more self-confident, independent, and unapologetic. She begins by taking characters such as Mrs. Jellyby or Harold Skimpole at face value and inhibiting her critical uneasiness about them. Her guardian tells her that Skimpole is childish goodness incarnate, and her initial reaction confirms this vision: "He was so full of feeling, too, and had such a delicate sentiment for what was beautiful or tender" (chap. 6). Yet her own acute observation eventually leads her to a very different and more accurate assessment and even allows her to understand why her guardian is taken in by Skimpole's "innocence." She is soon convinced that Skimpole's "display of guileless candour" was not as "artless as it seemed" (chap. 37). The same self-confidence and clear-sightedness are evident in her ability to judge other deceptive or deluded characters in the book accurately—Mrs. Jellyby, Mr. Turveydrop, Richard.

The blossoming of Esther's working intelligence is a continuous and uninterrupted process in the book. The same can hardly be said for her realization that she has a right to love and marry a man to whom she is attracted. Her romantic nature is much more completely crushed than her intelligence, in this case with the complicity of her guardian and her closest friends. It is surprising that her need for a lover has survived at all, in no matter how buried a form; but that it is very much alive despite all discouragement is evident for the first time when Mr. Guppy proposes. Esther's reaction to the offer of marriage from this absurd and vulgar man is totally unexpected yet, I think, completely convincing. She is anything but grateful, and her decisive rejection of him introduces a tone which we have never heard before in her words, and will seldom hear again: "Get up from that ridiculous position immediately, sir, or you will oblige me to break my implied promise and ring the bell!" (chap. 9).

The haughty dismissiveness and sheer command of these words sound more like Lady Dedlock than Esther Summerson. Esther here finds herself face-to-face with the kind of man who might be willing to take a piece of damaged goods, and her spirit rebels violently against the insult to her own pride. Her response suggests an extremely healthy sense of her own innocence and worth, a facet of her nature that is so regularly repressed that it can only declare its existence in such unexpected explosions. Esther's later reaction to the scene illustrates better than anything else in the novel how clearly Dickens connects adult with childhood experience:

> But, when I went upstairs to my own room, I surprised
> myself by beginning to laugh about it, and then surprised
> myself still more by beginning to cry about it. In short, I
> was in a flutter for a little while; and felt as if an old chord
> had been more coarsely touched than it ever had been since
> the days of the dear old doll, long buried in the garden.
>
> (chap. 9)

The doll had been the sole companion of her childhood, the
faithful listener to whom she could tell her troubles without fear of
rejection or reproach. When her godmother dies, she buries the doll
in the garden as if in penance. The ceremony reveals her guilt about
any form of self-indulgence, even such a sorry substitute for maternal acceptance. Its return in her fantasy at this moment shows how
Dickens uses childhood associations to explain adult behavior. For
the doll is a symbol of her "selfishness," her need for someone who
loves her absolutely. Faced with the prospect of the parody-lover
Mr. Guppy, the doll springs inevitably into her fantasy. It will not
stay buried, just as her adult truce with the past cannot altogether
prevent the occasional "coarse" reassertion of the primary feelings of
childhood.

Yet the pride and self-assertion evident in the scene with Guppy
desert her completely when she encounters a man to whom she is
fully attracted, Allan Woodcourt. It is at first impossible for her even
to acknowledge her interest. Her references to Woodcourt are in-
credibly tortured and coy; yet she is being neither "insincere" nor
girlishly silly. She is so terrified of losing him that she can hardly
bear to mention his existence. Her first reference to Woodcourt is
absurdly stilted and confused, especially for such a lucid and methodical narrator:

> I have omitted to mention in its place, that there was some
> one else at the family dinner party. It was not a lady. It was
> a gentleman. It was a gentleman of a dark complexion—a
> young surgeon. He was rather reserved, but I thought him
> very sensible and agreeable. At least, Ada asked me if I did
> not, and I said yes.
>
> (chap. 13)

This might be the "before" exhibit in a grammar book exercise on
how to construct complex sentences. Esther regularly becomes a

grammatical cripple whenever she mentions Woodcourt: "I believe—
at least I know—that he was not rich." "I think—I mean he told us—
that he had been in practice three or four years." "And so we gave
him our hands, one after another—at least, they did—and I did"
(chap. 17).

Her grammatical disarray is an expression of her anxiety. Deeply
convinced that her illegitimacy makes her unfit to marry a man of
worth, yet desperately hoping that the conviction is false, she turns
Woodcourt into a test case. To acknowledge her feeling for him is to
invite disappointment; hence the evasiveness and insincerity of prac-
tically everything she says about him until he actually proposes.
Since Woodcourt loves Esther, and since there are no real obstacles
to their marriage, one might have expected their romance to proceed
uninterrupted and Esther's self-confidence to grow as steadily as did
her trust in her own intelligence. But the plot presents two crucial
yet seemingly arbitrary setbacks: her illness and consequent disfigurement, and her guardian's proposal of marriage.

The effect of both these events is regressive. The loss of her
beauty convinces her that any thought of marriage is now out of the
question. The ambiguous phrase in her childhood vow, to "win
some love to myself if I could," must now be interpreted to mean
only the communal affection of those around her, not the romantic
love for which she longs. After seeing her new face in the mirror, she
tries desperately to convince herself to be satisfied with what she has.
This attempt clearly takes her back to an earlier stage, to her childhood vow:

> The childish prayer of that old birthday, when I had as-
> pired to be industrious, contented, and true-hearted, and
> to do good to some one, and win some love to myself if I
> could, came back into my mind with a reproachful sense of
> all the happiness I had since enjoyed, and all the affection-
> ate hearts that had been turned towards me. . . . I repeated
> the old childish prayer in its old childish words, and found
> that its old peace had not departed from it.
>
> (chap. 35)

But to rededicate oneself to an ideal formulated in childhood, particularly if it has already become a reality, is to make further progress
impossible. Esther is in fact ready to go beyond the vow at the
moment of her illness; but her disfigurement makes it impossible for

her to proceed. She seems trapped in the present and resigned to surrendering the future.

The treatment of Esther's illness is difficult to explain on the literal level: she loses and then regains her sight without explanation; her disfigured face is magically restored to its former beauty; Dickens even conspicuously avoids giving the illness a name. Yet as a symbol of Esther's psychological state at a particular moment in her development, it makes a good deal of sense. It comes when the circumstances of her birth—the fact that she is Lady Dedlock's child—are exposed. At about this point in the novel, her mother recognizes and reveals herself to the child she had long thought dead, and Mr. Tulkinghorn acquires the crucial piece of evidence that will make the facts public. The symbolic connection of these events with Esther's disfigurement seems clear. Her illegitimate birth is no longer a secret. She is made ugly in the eyes of the world. Her scarred face is the outward and visible sign of an inward and spiritual sin. Her two sharpest anxieties, about her birth and her disfigurement, come together in chapter 36 in which Lady Dedlock reveals herself and Ada sees her for the first time since her illness. Esther's violent reaction to her mother's revelation, which brings her to the nadir of her own self-confidence, feeds directly into her fear that Ada will not recognize her new face.

Her despair is suicidal. She is "possessed by a belief that it was right, and had been intended, that I should die in my birth; and that it was wrong, and not intended, that I should be then alive." And she reflects on "the new and terrible meaning of the old words, now moaning in my ears like a surge upon the shore, 'Your mother, Esther, was your disgrace, and you are hers. The time will come— and soon enough—when you will understand this better, and will feel it too, as no one save a woman can' " (chap. 36). It is as though the childhood curse had until this moment slept in her ear, for Esther has consistently evaded a fuller knowledge of the circumstances of her birth. But at this point in her life, when she stands at the threshold of maturity, the bare facts must be brought into the open and faced.

She recovers from the terrible despair into which her mother's revelation has thrown her, however, and the passage in which she declares her own innocence has often been quoted to suggest that her sense of confidence is fully restored. This seems to me a misinterpretation, though not an obvious one. Esther says: "I knew I was as innocent of my birth as a queen of hers; and that before my Heavenly Father I should not be punished for birth, nor a queen rewarded for it" (chap. 36). Although this has the ring of confidence, it should be noticed that Esther is planning to be vindicated in death, not in life. God will recognize her innocence and heaven will bring the rewards she has been denied on earth. But this reliance on a heavenly reward barely masks her despair about the possibility of earthly fulfillment. She has indeed already resigned herself to giving up Woodcourt *until* heaven where, she says, "I might aspire to meet him, *unselfishly, innocently, better far than he had thought me when I found some favour in his eyes, at the journey's end*" (chap. 35, italics added).

In such passages Esther tries to construct a possible life out of the elements of duty, selflessness, and the hope of a heavenly reward. She struggles to convince herself that they will do; but they will not. There is a strong intuitive awareness that these elements can only be oppressive if they are not combined with self-realization. These buried misgivings are brilliantly suggested during Esther's illness, as her fantasy takes over from her conscious mind. In her feverish reverie, she identifies her present household tasks with all the former duties of her life. The stream of reminiscence inevitably leads back to her godmother's house and oppresses her with the sense that every stage of her life, including the supposedly happy present, has merely presented her with a new set of "cares and difficulties." At this point she begins to hallucinate:

> I am almost afraid to hint at that time in my disorder—it seemed one long night, but I believe there were both nights and days in it—when I laboured up colossal staircases, ever striving to reach the top, and ever turned, as I have seen a worm in a garden path, by some obstruction, and labouring again. . . . I would find myself complaining "O more of these never-ending stairs, Charley,—more and more— piled up to the sky, I think!" and labouring on again.
>
> Dare I hint at that worse time when, strung together somewhere in great black space, there was a flaming necklace, or ring, or starry circle of some kind, of which *I* was one of the beads! And when my only prayer was to be taken off from the rest, and when it was such inexplicable agony and misery to be a part of the dreadful thing?
>
> (chap. 35)

In these dreams, Esther can no longer force herself to be content. The frustration of a life made up solely of duties is sharply expressed. Her obligations "mount up" like the endless staircases of her dream; there is no surmounting them in this life. The image of the starry circle probably expresses her intense though unacknowledged need to break out of the chain of commitments to the community, "to be taken off from the rest" and be a separate self. The whole passage is a powerful example of Dickens's use of fantasy, association, and dream to reveal elements in the psychological makeup of his characters that are systematically repressed in action and in speech.

Esther's illness (and the shame of her illegitimacy which is so closely related to it) has made her greatly more dependent on Mr. Jarndyce. As her obligations to her guardian increase, her sense of gratitude begins to mix with a kind of bleak helplessness. His protection envelops her; thanking him becomes a full-time duty, even a burden. Just before she reads Mr. Jarndyce's proposal of marriage, Esther exclaims, "I thanked him with my whole heart. What could I ever do but thank him!" (chap. 44). The question seems rhetorical but its answer is critical for her development. To spend her life in thanking Jarndyce is to surrender to the obstacle in her path.

Her guardian's proposal, coming at this point, is like Esther's illness, no arbitrary twist of the plot but a symbol of a particular moment in her development. The marriage would freeze her at the stage of filial dependence; she would be forever safe and adored. It is precisely because her relationship to Jarndyce has been a substitute for so much—a mother's love, a father's guidance, the sense of being accepted despite her birth—that it threatens to become her final human tie. But such sponsorship is a stage, hopefully leading to the child's sense of his own independent power and right of choice. If it lasts forever there has been a crucial failure in the educational process.

This, it seems to me, is the meaning of the proposal. The setback of her illness and the full revelation of her illegitimacy make Esther retreat to the safe world in which she knows she is loved. Yet when she realizes that the door may shut upon her there forever, she is profoundly disturbed. Her first reaction to Jarndyce's offer of marriage is far from joyous. She thinks of the proposal as the close of the benignant history I had been pursuing, and I felt that I had but one thing to do. To devote my life to his happiness was to thank him poorly, and what had I wished for the other night but some new means of thanking him?

Still I cried very much . . . as if something for which there was no name or distinct idea were indefinitely lost to me. I was very happy, very thankful, very hopeful; but I cried very much.

(chap. 44)

Esther sees her marriage to Jarndyce as an end, not a beginning, and she is convinced that she has no choice. ("I felt I had but one thing to do.") Although she does not understand exactly what she is giving up in accepting him, it becomes clear enough a few paragraphs later. Even after her illness she had kept some flowers that Woodcourt had given her, although she doubted then whether she had a right to keep them. Now they must be destroyed. She puts them for a moment to the lips of the sleeping Ada, recalls Ada's love for Richard, and then burns them. The ceremony is the first act of a novitiate.

Esther's deeply unsettled feelings about her engagement are also evident in her unwillingness to make it public. She delays as long as possible in telling anyone about it and then regularly insists on using the euphemism that she will become the mistress of Bleak House. The feeling that she is marrying the house rather than its owner is entirely appropriate. At the same time, Esther's busy cheerfulness begins to show signs of hysteria: "I resolved to be doubly diligent and gay. So I went about the house, humming all the tunes I knew; and I sat working and working in a desperate manner, and I talked and talked, morning, noon, and night" (chap. 1). Violent industry is Esther's characteristic response to misery she cannot acknowledge.

Yet even immersion in work will not allow her to ignore her fundamental need to be loved passionately rather than paternally. Her romantic longing has fastened on Woodcourt, and at this moment in her history he must therefore reappear. It is worth noting how many apparently arbitrary plot elements in Dickens are determined by his need for symbolic manifestations of internal states. When Esther sees Woodcourt again, she at first instinctively avoids his glance because she is "unwilling that he should see my altered looks." She has a strong impulse simply to run away, but she forces herself not to do so: "No, my dear, no. No, no, no!" (chap. 45). Her resistance is the first indication since her illness that her willpower can be used to confront her self-doubt rather than suppress it. Only very gradually does Woodcourt's love convince her that she is not hopelessly tainted, "disfigured," after all. When she is ready to entertain this radical idea, she is finally ready for his offer of marriage.

The proposal intensifies rather than resolves Esther's problems, however, because it confronts her with a need to choose when she is not yet psychologically ready to do so. She is still bound to her guardian. Her first response to the knowledge that she can be loved passionately, that there are in fact no obstacles to normal life for her, is not joy but violent regret: "O, too late to know it now, too late, too late. That was the first ungrateful thought I had. Too late" (chap. 61). Her natural impulse is rebellious. She feels that her engagement, her dependence on Jarndyce, fetters her, but the bond is too powerful for her to break.

She is terrified not of hurting Jarndyce but of pleasing herself. Nothing in her childhood or young adulthood has prepared her to think she has a right to do so. After her first uncontrollably bitter reaction, Esther can only allow herself to use Woodcourt's proposal as a way of fulfilling her childhood vow: "He had called me the beloved of his life, and had said I would be evermore as dear to him as I was then; and *I felt as if my heart would not hold the triumph of having heard those words.* My first wild thought had died away. It was not too late to hear them, for *it was not too late to be animated by them to be good, true, grateful, and contented*" (chap. 61, italics added). Her "selfish" impulse is immediately translated into duty, and she can only think of ways to make herself worthy of Woodcourt's faith. It is impossible for her to assume that she already *is* worthy; all her plans are for self-improvement.

The effect of such contradictory impulses can only be paralysis. The need to depend on her guardian and the need to break away from him seem equally strong. Yet a few pages later, the conflict has been mysteriously resolved and Esther is married to Woodcourt. This conclusion to Esther's history seems to me sheer fantasy. Everything in her narrative has stressed the potent nature of her conflicts and the feebleness of her own will in dealing with them. Indeed, she must not even allow herself to acknowledge them. Such a situation demands a tragic ending—or a deus ex machina. Dickens chooses the latter. Esther's decision is made for her by Jarndyce, who surrenders her to Woodcourt without even consulting her. The whole scene is dominated by magical and fantastic elements whose function is to dissolve the contradictions inherent in the situation. Where conflict was, there harmony shall be.

All the plans for Esther's future life deny the presence of conflict or the necessity of exclusive choice. The house where she and Woodcourt will live was purchased and furnished by her guardian. It too is to be called Bleak House, so that Esther will be its mistress after all. It is decorated inside and out like her old home and will even have a replica of the Growlery, where her guardian plans to spend much of his time. Esther had hoped to be vindicated by God, and it is notable that Jarndyce becomes indistinguishable from a benevolent Providence in the book's concluding section. He denies the part of himself which had once wanted her as a wife: "I am your guardian and your father now" (chap. 64). Esther sees him in a new way: "As I sat looking fixedly at him, and the sun's rays descended, softly shining through the leaves, upon his bare head, I felt as if the brightness on him must be like the brightness of the Angels" (chap. 64). Such religious references relate to the Ada-Richard plot, which comes to a tragic conclusion simultaneously, and in which it is made clear that *only* eternity can resolve the conflicts of earthly life: "A smile irradiated his face, as she bent to kiss him. He slowly laid his face down upon her bosom, drew his arms closer round her neck, and with one parting sob began the world. Not this world, O not this! The world that sets this right" (chap. 65).

The treatment of Esther's internal conflicts has been so detailed, painstaking, and psychologically plausible that the sudden miraculous resolution, in which fantasy elements are presented within a realistic framework, seems totally unconvincing. Yet several critics have treated the change in Esther as a triumphant self-assertion. J. Hillis Miller, for example, writes of "her liberation into an authentic life when she chooses to accept the self she finds herself to be." I can see no such existential choice. Esther cannot properly be said to choose at all, and much of her old self manages to survive her change of situation. This is illustrated obliquely and symbolically in Ada's return to Jarndyce after Richard's death. Esther has treated Ada as a second self throughout the novel, but they are really alternative aspects of a single nature. Esther's marriage to Woodcourt is possible only after Ada loses her husband and returns to her loving guardian.

The two girls change places. Only one of them can venture into the world of love and marriage at a time; the alter ego must stay at home. The psychological complexity of the book is often revealed in such symbolic ways just when the literal events seem least plausible and convincing. In the interstices of Dickens's magical solution, he cannot help planting these grains of truth.

Dickens characteristically resorts to fantasy whenever his sharp eye for human suffering has uncovered more than he can bear to contemplate. His detailed realistic observation stops short at the borders of despair. The resolution of the Esther plot is only one case in point. There are two other significant instances of a resort to fantasy in the book, the first of which also involves Esther. I have tried to show how psychologically plausible Dickens's portrait is, but there is one crucial fact this analysis has ignored: that a child brought up in a totally loveless home, as Esther was, is almost surely doomed to grow up unable to love anyone. Yet Esther is an open, affectionate, thoroughly responsive person. Here Dickens's realism comes into conflict with his desire to present his victims as purely victimized. The portrait of the bitter Miss Wade in *Little Dorrit* suggests that he knew how unlovable a person who had never been loved could be; but Miss Wade is a minor character, not the heroine of the novel, and we are not asked to waste very much sympathy on her. Esther, on the other hand, is an example of Dickens's myth of the innocent child, whose goodness must be absolute. Her harsh upbringing can leave her incomplete and vulnerable, but not selfish or corrupt. Dickens's vision of society depends on the idea of victimization, on the absolute separation of the oppressors from the oppressed. That the oppressed can go on to become oppressors in their turn is an example of the sort of pessimistic conclusion his fantasy exists to deny.

The same element of fantasy enters into his resolution of the sociopolitical plot of *Bleak House*. Here Dickens comes much closer to acknowledging the darkness of his own vision, which has led Jo, Lady Dedlock, Tulkinghorn, Gridley, and Richard to their deaths. The institution of Chancery goes on. The government remains in the same incompetent hands. The Church and the charitable organizations are as corrupt as ever. All this can hardly be called a retreat from pessimism into fantasy. Yet the book ends not in London but in Eden, where a small group of good and permanently innocent people transform the new Bleak House into a community of love existing outside the blighted world described in the rest of the novel. As Dickens's satire becomes more savage, his need to invent an escape from the world he satirizes becomes more desperate and increasingly forces him to resort to fantasy.

It is possible that the myths he characteristically uses—the innocent child, the pure victim, the community of the saved, the good rich man, etc.—gave him the courage to describe his society with much greater fidelity and candor. The promise of an ultimate escape in fantasy from the black world of the novel may well have unlocked his ability to describe its misery—both social and psychological—in such extraordinary and vivid detail. If this is so, then the savage indictment of social institutions in *Bleak House,* as well as the detailed psychological realism of the portrait of Esther, are both dependent on the element of fantasy at the borders of each.

Confusion and Consciousness in Dickens's Esther

Judith Wilt

Dickens wrote three fictional autobiographies; in one he made himself a woman. This was dangerous magic, and the book strove against him rather more than he looked for. Yet the rewards were substantial, and in one respect, I believe, supreme. Giving over his pen to the female writer of *Bleak House,* he found he could not relax into the simple narcissism of his male avatars, for whom the question "whether I am the hero of my own life" fills most of the horizon. Instead he found himself committed to the wider anxieties of the Self-Other relationship, which are the female's lot in the world. In instinctive direct address to the Other, in that imaginative impingement on and of "my unknown friend," Dickens's Esther Summerson shows him a new kind of horizon, and in so doing, liberates in the book's other, sister, voice, the most profoundly direct address to the aggregate Other, "ladies and gentlemen born with Heavenly compassion in your hearts," that he was ever to make.

Sister voice? Why not? Esthers don't get angry but Deborahs do. The Charles Dickens who dined with Jane and Thomas Carlyle might consciously have reached for the tones of an Isaiah *or* a Cassandra; and the voice of the unnamed narrator of *Bleak House,* goaded beyond confusion and hurt to the certainties of the Victorian Prophetic Sublime, sounds to my ears the very note of Cassandra. This suggests perhaps a new gestalt in the shape of *Bleak House,* not a loud giant male narrator hatching a soft "little woman," but a

From *Nineteenth Century Fiction* 32, no. 3 (December 1977). © 1977 by the Regents of the University of California.

mortal female, unbottling, on occasion, a Genius, a superb Artifice, and flying it like a kite, like James's balloon of Romance. Not two opposites but two phases of one being, two deployed strategies for living in the fog.

The Genius is surely a gorgeous Fairy. Quivering with outrage, ripe with judgment, she can grasp our worst nightmare, stalking Famine, and use it upon us without fear; she can hold us to our oldest, most fragile hope through torment without pity:

> "Our Father!—yes, that's wery good, sir." . . .
> "Art in Heaven—is the light a-comin, sir?" . . .
> "Hallowed be—thy—"
> The light is come upon the dark benighted way. Dead!

She is the living image of our power of attack upon Unrighteousness and throws off splendors of language like a firestick:

> All the mirrors in the house are brought into action now: many of them after a long blank. They reflect handsome faces, simpering faces, youthful faces, faces of threescore-and-ten that will not submit to be old; the entire collection of faces that have come to pass a January week or two at Chesney Wold, and which the fashionable intelligence, a mighty hunter before the Lord, hunts with a keen scent, from their breaking cover at the Court of St. James's to their being run down to Death.

Outrage and judgment, power and attack are often desirable responses to injustice and corruption. This essay, however, proposes to explore the possibilities of strategic confusion, Esther's resourceful refusal to close in on judgment.

I

This paradox opens again perhaps the oldest unresolved quarrel about *Bleak House,* the quarrel over the "reality" of Esther Summerson's character and the nature of Dickens's intentions regarding her narrative. Beginning her final section, Esther greets again "the unknown friend to whom I write" and hopes for some "dear remembrance . . . his or hers." He responded disappointingly. Typical are John Forster's rather curt dismissal of her "too conscious unconsciousness," or The *Spectator*'s breezy assumption that the kind of "girl" Esther was supposed to be "would not write her own memoirs." More recently Morton Dauwen Zabel has been unable to connect the "simple, virtuous, and naïve intelligence" with the "insights of a sophisticated kind," which unaccountably make their way into Esther's narrative; and her "mock-modesty" he finds merely "one of the tiresome features of her tale."

Criticism has the same difficulty with Esther's modesty, interestingly, as it does with Clarissa's chastity, a difficulty with three main strands: (1) virtuous consciousness of one's own virtue is technically a hard trick to pull off in life or in fiction; (2) such virtuous consciousness is doubly hard to establish validly in a first-person narrative in which the modern reader has come to look greedily, as Henry James phrased it, for the "terrible *fluidity* of self-revelation"; and (3) virtuous consciousness of women's virtue has always been reserved to men—women ought to be asleep on that suit.

Uriah Heep gave "umility" a very bad name, of course, but it is a virtue nevertheless; it is the virtue by which one knows and contacts the mixed grandeur of the world. Pride, which David and Pip seek, is the virtue by which one knows and contacts the often bitterly mixed grandeur of the self. At the end of *David Copperfield* the hero of his own life pictures himself dying, or closing his narrative (the same thing), and the last face to fade is that of the modest Agnes, "pointing upward!" That which points outwards and upwards, archetypal shape of woman, is now recognized as properly part of the shape of the whole person, who adds to this the inward supporting shape which is self-love. Esther Summerson's desire, kindled when she is yet a schoolchild by the awful experience of having her birthday wiped out of the calendar of her solitary home, shapes itself in this double supporting and supportive form, "to do some good to some one, and win some love if I could," that is, win the right to others' love and to her own self-love. Like all Dickens's children she was cruelly tried and "bent" before the dawn of consciousness, but along that bias she chooses a full and flexible shape—which promotes alike the doing and the winning, the loving and being loved, the seeing and the being recognized.

At the end of *Bleak House,* Esther settles down to living, declines to close her narrative (the same thing). The narrative leaves in unprecedented suspension, neither made nor contradicted, the statement by which the self kills the world—"I am beautiful." Don't you know you are beautiful? Esther's husband asks on the last page, "laughing," as if such knowledge were a light thing to hold. And the woman, after hundreds of pages of witness rich with experience of love-worthy things inside and outside herself, instinctively seeks the grammar of suspension, within which an imperfect "yes" to his question coexists with an imperfect "yes" to her own: "I did not know that; I am not certain that I know it now. But I know that [those outside me] are very beautiful . . . and that they can very well do without much beauty in me—even supposing——"

Critics tend to write about *Bleak House* as if the novel concluded restfully in the typical Dickensian personal pastorale, as if Bleak House were Dingley Dell, when in fact the suspension—grammatical, dramatic, and psychological—of the novel's final lines, final statement, responds fully to the common complaint, put most clearly perhaps by Barbara Hardy, that personal rest does not really answer public unrest. "The conclusion," Hardy argues, "is only partially responsive to the rest of the novel, squeezes its solace through too narrow an exit. . . . I am not suggesting that Esther should be given more 'opposition' . . . but that Dickens should conclude with some indication of his opposition since it has created so much in the whole world of the novel." She wants Dickens to end the novel as it began, with the voice of opposition, but the decision to end, suspend, with the unrestful voice of the private world seems a more subtle way to suggest, not conclusive opposition, but the confusion which, as a positive and negative quality, lies at the heart of the narrative.

Put to the task of narrative, Esther chooses her proper syntactic shapes: to know and teach those outside towards whom she is pointed, and to know and regulate her own knowing. Her personal syntactic shape is the parenthetical sentence; and the closer her knowing comes to herself, the thicker become the parentheses, which signal the strain and confusion of knowing her knowing. Even in small matters she keeps watch over the accuracy of her expressions of knowing: her godmother was "handsome; and if she had ever smiled, would have been (I used to think) like an angel"; her godmother imposed a soul-eating quarantining of her, as if she had been a disease, as early as "the first week of my going to the school (I remember it very well)." And in large matters, given that Esther is committed to the exposures (hazily protected) of the parentheses, she does, entertainingly, confusedly, the best she can, like us all: "I have mentioned that, unless my vanity should deceive me (as I know it may, for I may be very vain, without suspecting it—though indeed I don't), my comprehension is quickened when my affection is." Protected similarly—that is inadequately—by the dash, Esther exposes again and again the anxious knowing of her early knowing: "I never could be unrestrained with her—no, could never even love her as I wished"; and of her early unknowing: "And so [the doll] used to sit propped up in a great arm-chair, with her beautiful complexion and rosy lips, staring at me—or not so much at me, I think, as at nothing—while I busily stitched away, and told her every one of my secrets."

Recognizing that she once needed to be seen by the doll and now can see, quietly, the doll seeing Nothing, without identifying herself as Nothing, is, we discover, one of Esther's crucial pieces of knowing. The doll's imagined loving gaze sustained, the doll's painted beauty confirmed, the existence of these qualities in a world which only Esther's matching qualities could have intuited possessed them, so steadfastly did that world, manipulated by the godmother, return a perfectly blank response to Esther's regard. When Miss Barbary dies, her carved face immovable and unsoftened, Esther entreats that face for "the least sign that she knew or heard me." To look upon that world-face and see it reflect nothing of oneself, and yet to feel bound in the deepest part of one's Victorian woman's self to win from it some picture of its/our face expressive of love is to know terror and desperation.

On the other hand, to look too long is to lock the self, mesmerized, into that imaged state of nonbeing—whether by the weakness of surrender or by the hard strength of the Barbary sisters, Esther's mother, and her godmother, who return that world-blankness a defiant tragic human blankness. Esther's supreme moral danger, we discover slowly, is not in that too conscious consciousness which destroys virtue, nor even in the apparent refusal to credit her own quality; it is in the inheritance she carries from her female relations of blankness and willed solitude. Lady Dedlock calls her affliction Boredom, but it is Boredom of truly monstrous proportions, a catastrophic personal blankness, outfacing a blank world with no child or lover in it to return one's featured face. When Esther recognizes her godmother's face, and her own, in the cold profile of the Lady of Chesney Wold, a deep distress, a true Nausea, claims her. That distress is consummated on the day of mutual recognition in the forest, when the daughter beats at that blankness to be let in, to be allowed to help—to show her mother the figured, if from another point of view, pox-scarred face of the world, and restore to her her own figured, scarred, living face—and is refused:

> "The dark road I have trodden for so many years will end where it will. I follow it alone to the end, whatever the end be. . . ."
> "Dear mother, are you so resolved?"
> "I *am* resolved. I have long outbidden folly with folly, pride with pride, scorn with scorn, insolence with insolence, and have outlived many vanities with many more."

> "We shall meet no more. . . . If you hear of Lady Dedlock, brilliant, prosperous, and flattered; think of your wretched mother, conscience-stricken, underneath that mask! Think that the reality is in her suffering, in her useless remorse, in her murdering within her breast the only love and truth of which it is capable! And then forgive her, if you can; and cry to Heaven to forgive her, which it never can!"

In this sense, Esther's mother is "Lady Dedlock: Murderess," as the notes arriving at the Dedlock home insist; she has murdered not her enemy, the pursuing lawyer Tulkinghorn, but her love, her bond to the world, her child, and herself.

Lady Dedlock is one of Dickens's great tragic characters in her own right, linked from one perspective with the Rosa Dartles, the Miss Wades, the Estellas, who have made their fearful accommodation of a passionate self with a coldly hostile world by means of a terrible strength of will, turning themselves to stone, brooking neither injury nor aid, surrendering to the Giant Despair. But she is preeminently important as Esther's mother, as the long blank shadow upon the autobiographical narrator of *Bleak House*. And as we look at Dickens's three autobiographical narrators, their similarities and differences, this fact stands out provocatively—the young men move almost without check into solitude and self-regard, easily gliding out from the vague shadows of weak or absent parents, but Dickens's venture into female autobiography found him creating for her nemesis and conciliation the strongest mother, the greatest Solitaire, in all the crowded canvas of his world.

II

David Copperfield, Esther Summerson, and Philip Pirrip are all orphans in a world crowded with half-parents and substitute parents; each is thus formed in a "household" rather than in a family. Each has for this reason a preconscious but powerful sense that he or she *holds place* mysteriously, and perhaps even criminally. When Esther notes in the middle of her narrative that "so strangely did I hold my place in this world, that . . . I had never, to my own mother's knowledge . . . borne a name," she registers this sense of the instability of place and the need to grip for it, as well as that curious instability of name and the need to invent it, which marks all these narrators, and in some sense initiates their autobiographies.

Autobiographers must lay claim, as part of their technical donnée, their authority, to a near miraculous power of observation and memory, and then to an overwhelming pressure or purpose-of-writing to account for the deliberate conjuring up of this power as text. It is David Copperfield, Dickens's first autobiographer, who makes the simplest, the Wordsworthian argument for the special observantness of a certain kind of person: "I believe the power of observation in numbers of very young children to be quite wonderful for its closeness and accuracy. Indeed, I think that most grown men who are remarkable in this respect, may with greater propriety be said not to have lost the faculty, than to have acquired it." Esther Summerson adds another, a Shelleyan dimension to this argument: "I had always rather a noticing way . . . a silent way of noticing what passed before me, and thinking I should like to understand it better. I have not by any means a quick understanding. When I love a person very tenderly indeed, it seems to brighten." And Pip adds a final, a dramatic, perhaps a Byronic, dimension in the brilliant opening page of *Great Expectations,* which traces all significant observation back to a single traumatic confrontation with "a fearful man," during which the self first knows itself sundered, somehow criminally, from all the supporting environment of land, sea, and people with which the self was once merged. This criminal-birth trauma is rendered memorably at closer quarters in *David Copperfield* when the young boy watches sold at auction the caul born with him, and the sight of that once living environment, that former "part of myself" now fallen away, touches him with dread.

Incidents like this testify to the impressive power of Not-Love, of Guilt, Dread, Hostility, Resentment, to quicken the observation and understanding. Esther has this power, as well as that of Affection, to quicken her, just as David, through Peggotty, and Pip, through Joe, retain as a quickening power, along with their Animus, that sense of unsought and undeserved Natural Love which animates their best understandings. This power survives, though it is weakened in the two boys by their clear perception of Peggotty's and Joe's comparative helplessness against the Murdstones and the Mrs. Joes of the world.

Esther's dramatic recognition of criminal self-separation and the death of the not-self comes, like David's and Pip's, in an early confrontation with a fearful person of her own sex. She sees the words written on her godmother's face: "It would have been far better, little Esther, that you had had no birthday; that you had never been born!" And her instinctive response is, "O, dear godmother, tell me, pray do tell me, did mama die on my birthday? . . . What did I do to her? . . . why is it my fault?" Indeed, deprived as she is of any ally in her early life, traumatized by the conviction that her birth was a criminal usurpation, not of a sister's (i.e., David) or a brother's (i.e., Pip), but of a mother's life, deeply frightened by her own coldness to her godmother and Mrs. Rachel, even more than by theirs toward her, it is only remarkable that any power of Affection at all was created in Esther, let alone that it was, as it clearly is, primary. Noting the almost ostentatious absence of a Peggotty or a Joe, the substitution in Esther's case of long chats with her doll, long silent communing with her shadow walking home from school, one cannot help but see Dickens picturing the girl child mysteriously, Originally, free from, or resisting, outward communications in this respect, spinning Love out of her own substance.

Esther's power of Animus, that self-protective Critical power, does in fact quickly rise in accompaniment to offer its alarming observations and quicken her to dreadful understanding. But this power is weaker, and its communications are not hidden or erased but monitored, deployed in a special strategy that holds the power just at the threshold of consciousness, that holds critical analysis just at the point before the irretrievable and damaging separation of elements occurs, that holds judgment in the doorway between bewildered recognition and certainty. Deployed thus, the power is not Animus exactly, but that great and holy and fruitful power, Confusion. Esther's narrative is the cry Confusion—not Damnation—to the evils of the world and the enemies of love.

Giving oneself to this power has advantages both human and narrative (some disadvantages, too, of course). Humanly, Esther need never fully credit or participate in that wrenching separation of the self from the world; her relationship with it has thus the intimacy of a system, mutually nourishing (or perishing). Narratively, as I hope to show, her power to resist closing in on judgment has advantages too. The price, of course, is harboring the world's confusion in her own system, being, as she testifies over and over, confused. As a positive strategy for living life, this has affinities with that strategy of art Keats called negative capability—the ability to rest, occasionally in doubt, without that "restless" willful seeking of the conviction that sunders, the definition that destroys.

Esther's Confusion is deployed to allow her to keep active, to "do some good," and to win and give love. In the most paralyzing atmosphere of malice, pride, ignorance, and brutality, it allows her to be effective and to promote active affection, for instance, in Caddy Jellyby and Prince Turveydrop, where a direct, critical look by them at Mrs. Jellyby's myopic incompetence or Mr. Turveydrop's selfishness would have ended in hostility, ridicule, impotence, madness, or worse. Caddy's initial passionate "I wish Africa was dead" promises incipient matricide, and understandably enough too, but Esther holds, and holds her to, a balanced sympathy and understanding and disapproval in fusion, confusion, carrying Caddy back with her from that dangerous edge where judgment becomes Godlike. On all the significant and tragic issues in the story, from Jo and the national smallpox to Richard and his deadly gambler's virus, from the outermost limits of Chancery to the middle distance of her life where Jarndyce and Skimpole and Mrs. Pardiggle contest the meaning of charity and of will, to the innermost Gordian knot of her own identity, Esther holds fast to her Confusion, lest fear or anger or frustration or condemnation subvert her other, major power, her Affection.

If she needed an example of the subversions of fear, she has it before her in Jo, the vagabond from Tom-all-Alone's back slum, who has been "moved on" and "shuffled off" from his miserable holes so many times by a hostile or indifferent world that even when he is finally taken in by the brickmaker's wife, by Charley, and by Esther herself, and lodged in the unmistakable strong heart of love and care, a word from the formidable Inspector Bucket is enough to frighten him out again, eventually to his death. Hearing this appalling inhumanity from the man who is now spending days and nights aiding her in trying to save her mother's life is so trying to Esther that Confusion amounting almost to unconsciousness is needed to go on with him on her errand: "Although I remember this conversation now, my head was in confusion at the time, and my power of attention hardly did more than enable me to understand that he entered into these particulars to divert me." And if Esther needed an example of the subversion of love by angry frustration, she has it before her in Richard Carstone, ward and possible heir in Jarndyce and Jarndyce, whose naïve expectation of the best from himself and from the case turns to a soul-numbing paranoia and suspicion even of his supporters, a power, like Jo's fear, making straight for Death in spite of all that his love for his cousin Ada can put into the scales on the side of life.

Richard, like Ada and Esther, started out in a state of benign confusion about the nature of Chancery and the world, and of benign passivity about it. His head "ached with wondering how it happened, if men were neither fools nor rascals; and my heart ached to think they could possibly be either," but "Chancery will work none of its bad influences on *us,*" he is certain. Esther is certain of nothing, ever, except of her comparative smallness in the larger world and of the presence, foglike and often obscure, of some rag of goodness in the fools and rascals, some glint of Divinity in the wretched scenes around, some finger of Providence in the miserable events she must register in her "noticing" way and must somehow love, if her understanding of them is ever to quicken. In this mode she notices the simple beauty of the Lord Chancellor's gold lace, the "courtly and kind" manner, the "affable and polite" sensitivity that accompanies his "searching look" and brisk dismissal, the casual but accurate understanding of Richard's need to be spoken to, standing man to man, "as if he still knew, though he *was* Lord Chancellor, how to go straight to the candour of a boy." This sound and solid human being is the same man that another observer, or the same observer in another mode, earlier descried sitting "with a foggy glory round his head, softly fenced in with crimson cloth and curtains," carrying on the traditional jokes about Jarndyce and Jarndyce, and "dexterously" vanishing when addressed by the ruined man from Shropshire about whose existence the Chancellor must affect to be "legally ignorant . . . after making it desolate for a quarter of a century."

That these are the same man, that the same being who professionally abetted the legal erasure of the man from Shropshire added personal graces to the legal establishment of Richard in Jarndyce's Court Wardship, does add up to a monstrous moral maze, the same one Dickens pictures again, sinisterly, comically, in the schizophrenic Wemmick of *Great Expectations.* In court later on to observe the case of Jarndyce and Jarndyce with new connections to it through her love for Richard and Ada and John Jarndyce, Esther notices even more, and understands even better, but holds to her Confusion: "this was so curious and self-contradictory to me, who had no experience of it, that it was at first incredible, and I could not comprehend it." Another observer, or the same one in a different mode, drives impatiently and sarcastically past Confusion to clarification: "The one great principle of the English law is, to make business for itself. There is no other principle distinctly, certainly, and consistently maintained through all its narrow turnings. Viewed by this light it becomes a coherent scheme, and not the monstrous maze the laity are apt to think it."

Admirably clear, wonderfully satisfying, this narrative captures the very pith of our observation in this mode. Still, is it the truth? Probably not. Bitter as it is for a proud and caring man or woman to accept, melioration, grumbling, confusion, maze, and fog hit closer to the truth of being and even the truth of effective action than the certainties and clarities of Revolutionary condemnation. Dickens unmistakably shifted to this truth every time condemnation began to work itself out in his fictions; the treatments of historical revolutions in *Barnaby Rudge* and *A Tale of Two Cities* are the clearest examples. What truly fascinated him was the mystery of self-contradiction, of "foggy glory." That is why, even of the two characters who belong especially to the narrative's unnamed observer (or the same one in her different mode), the most subtle pains are taken, not with the mud-boy Jo, who instinctively fears, but with the fog-brain Sir Leicester Dedlock, who instinctively loves. Full of foolish and destructive certainties as he is about everything else, the old man calls steadfastly upon the power of Confusion in order to keep on loving his dishonored lady after the exposure of her illegitimate motherhood and the suspicions surrounding the death of her tormentor Tulkinghorn cause her to fly. Confusion garbles his tongue and disables his mind and body, enabling him to communicate the single proper response confused humans have to make to and of each other: "Full forgiveness. Find————." As with Esther's, and the novel's final broken-off communication, as with Jo's final prayer, "Hallowed be—thy—," it is neither necessary nor desirable to complete, and thus circumscribe and limit, the thought.

As an exploration of the mystery of self-contradiction, *Bleak House* is in fact less seriously engaged with the problem of the law, which is anyhow a secondary and suspect activity of the human heart, than it is with the problem of charity, with the disturbing contradictions of that primary virtue which is "the greatest of these." Esther finds that charity, in its organized form, as practiced by Mrs. Jellyby, Mr. Quale, and Mrs. Gusher, has turned into a ritual for the mutual stroking of its practitioners: "nothing respecting them was half so clear to us, as that it was Mr. Quale's mission to be in ecstasies with everybody else's mission, and that it was the most popular mission of all." About this relatively minor contradiction of charity's self she can be clear enough. She finds too that charity in its religiously oriented, hence class-oriented, form, as practiced by Mrs. Pardiggle and Mr. Chadband, has this contradiction and another, more painful one—it cannot be effective where it is most needed, with the poor. The brilliant early scene in the brickmaker's cottage, where, even as his baby dies, the brutal and proud husband rejects religion and charity because it comes at the price of being taken into "religious custody," is a superb example of Esther's insight, quickened by the anxiety of an affection rejected. Her discomfort, and Ada's, is profound, but her bewilderment is only partial: "We both felt painfully sensible that between us and these people there was an iron barrier, which could not be removed by our new friend. By whom, or how, it could be removed, we did not know; but we knew that." Unlike all the other charitable people in the novel, Esther knows the limitations of her knowing.

One is driven back by such contradictions to the exercise of pure charity without the sanction of organized religion and even without the logic of desert, driven back, as John Jarndyce is, to the refreshment of undesigning charity to the undesigning, to Harold Skimpole. This is the locus of Esther's classic, her supreme deployment of the power of Confusion to arrest at the threshold the slide towards despair or hatred. That is to say, if Harold Skimpole is, in all his terrifying parasitic splendor, all his cold articulate geniality, innocent of design, then Jarndyce and Esther are bound in charity to support him, and to watch and despair as he gaily pulls out the last prop from under the wretched bill collector Coavinses, the fleeing Jo, the expiring Richard. If he does it consciously, he is a true monster of selfishness, one of Dickens's greatest, and must be closed in on and crushed. John Jarndyce, his patron, insists nervously that Skimpole is an irresponsible child. Inspector Bucket, hardened and perhaps simplified by years of contact with the multitude of human scam artists, is certain Skimpole is a conscious manipulator. Esther, who knows a minor league vampire when she sees one, in lawyer Vholes, for instance, remains steadfastly Confused about Skimpole's motives from first to last.

She notices right away (we are to trust her in this as we do about the Lord Chancellor, I think) his quite considerable attractions, his musical and drawing talents, his capacity to knit together the company in relaxed sparkling talk, "a perfect charm . . . free from effort and spontaneous . . . great humour . . . delightful gaiety . . . so full of feeling" and most perniciously fascinating of all, "the frankest manner." "Candour" is the deadliest tool in the arsenal of the guiltless man—he must feel no participation in Original Sin who uses it "vivaciously." With his candor, Skimpole locks the charitable man and the loving woman into the tightest of philosophic vises: "All he asked of society was, to let him live. *That* wasn't much" and tightens the screws unmercifully:

> It's only you, the generous creatures, whom I envy. . . . I envy you your power of doing what you do. It is what I should revel in, myself. I don't feel any vulgar gratitude to you. I almost feel as if *you* ought to be grateful to *me,* for giving you the opportunity of enjoying the luxury of generosity. I know you like it.

Charity needs its object, from the point of view of pure logic, pure observation of life's mechanic (" 'In fact, that is our family department,' said Mr. Skimpole, 'in this hurly-burly of life. We are capable of looking on and of being interested, and we *do* look on, and we *are* interested.' ") Skimpole is virtually unanswerable here. He is the inevitable second inhabitant of Bleak House; he exists in order, by foil, to support the claims of others to be charitable, efficacious, and wise; his long exposition of why he could not undermine Bucket's methods or Bucket's trust in the corruptibility of men by refusing his bribe to tell the whereabouts of Jo is masterful. His effect upon persons, tête-à-tête, is like magic, perfectly convincing; only out of his presence can a coolness, a doubt, take root: "The more I saw of him, the more unlikely it seemed to me, when he was present, that he could design, conceal, or influence anything; and yet the less likely that appeared when he was not present, and the less agreeable it was to think of his having anything to do with any one for whom I cared," says Esther. From his emptily sane perspective, he is correct in the sentence he writes in his posthumous memoirs: "Jarndyce, in common with most other men I have known, is the incarnation of selfishness," and Esther, from her richly confused perspective, is right to close that book immediately. Even uncommercialized charity has its modicum of guilt, for it is an act of will, and will is the most confusing of human virtues to the Victorians.

The truth is, that by the measure by which Jarndyce is the incarnation of selfishness, Skimpole is the incarnation of selflessness. He denies that he has will, though he playfully admires this quality in Jarndyce and Esther: "You are ready at all times to go anywhere, to do anything. Such is Will! I have no Will at all—and no Won't—simply Can't." He is indeed the *object* of charity; by his own account an object to the spectator in himself. Esther is fascinated and confused by *this* mystery in him above all; he speaks of himself "as if he were not at all his own affair." He is one in the system of "things lazily adapt[ing] themselves to purposes" as Skimpole sees the system, an irresponsible part of the "scheme of things that A should squint to make B happier in looking straight; or that C should carry a wooden leg, to make D better satisfied with his flesh and blood in a silk stocking." Skimpole is in this way constantly shaking the foundation of self-esteem as Esther knows it. The ultimate self-contradiction, he contrives to make the existence of will, the making of oneself one's own affair, and of affairs, to some extent, one's own, seem faintly ridiculous, faintly reprehensible.

And so, of course, it is. Faintly.

Nevertheless, beyond any permanent damage from ridicule, or even from error, Esther knows that affairs *are* hers, and more, ridiculous and reprehensible as it sometimes seems, she is her own affair. With no mother or father, how can it be otherwise? Being her own affair, Esther makes what adjustments she can. The "submission, self-denial, diligent work" enjoined by her godmother, she translates, through the power of affection, into "industrious, contented, and kind-hearted." Set apart from the human joys of an unshadowed woman, she yet instinctively avoids the self-congratulatory solitude of those "good" women, Miss Barbary and Mrs. Rachel. She will strive to engage with men and women and to accept the guilt of that intimacy. The hardness of this choice, either "goodness" in solitude or error in company, brings tears to the narrating Esther's eyes, even as she writes of her life's first significant event. She is "very cheerful," but the position is still hard and the tears still come. This narrator has not entirely stabilized; she oscillates in the present, as she has always done, between a dreamy tranced stare at the isolating shadow on her, on life, and a resistance to that stare, a shaking of herself awake—"There! I have wiped them away now, and can go on again properly."

In one area of her life, of course, the trance almost claims her; the other side of the independent, active, old-maidish identity she chooses is that of sexual sleep, a self-contradiction half known to her through the bouts of tears that come every time she resists marriage proposals and fancies, even Guppy's. Her marriage with Alan Woodcourt (actually one of the more convincing of Dickens's male lovers, with his penetrating silences, his quiet conflicts, and the curious strength connected with his "professional interest in death") is her reward both for loyalty to that first promise to marry Jarndyce and for the confused loyalty of her intuition that in agreeing to this sexless marriage she was somehow being "remiss."

In another area the trance is resolutely fought: her sense that she is the embodiment of her mother's disgrace and therefore ought to be even more isolated than her mother, she confines to dreams or to momentary paralyzed daydreams from which she can shake herself awake with an alarm-bell ring of the housekeeping keys. At Chesney Wold, however, now nearly twenty-one, woman looks into woman's eyes, sees kinship, and yet cannot fully touch it. The nightmare barriers are there in the flesh: Lady Dedlock, frozen almost to nonbeing in self-contempt, feels forced to reject Esther and go her way alone; and Esther experiences herself concretely as "the sword of Damocles," the murderer of her mother she was born to be. At twenty, with a lifetime of highhearted discipline and intelligent noticing to draw on, one can cope, almost, even with this. The dreams disappear from the narrative, replaced by a cruel but conscious "augmented terror of myself," which can be fought in the open with reason and faith and hope. Fought, but never entirely erased; much of the anxiety in the present time of Esther's narrative, noticeable every time she dwells for long on her own feelings and trials, reflects this bedrock terror: that by announcing her existence she would kill her mother.

And yet, of course, she cannot fail to announce her existence, nor can she really accept separation from her mother, even though real-izing the connection is, as her mother shows her the situation, the final destructive act. Nor can she accept identification with her mother. Even Confusion is not entirely adequate to the situation in the final third of the novel; with an inner life full of thoughts of her guilty mother and her guilty self, an outer behavior strategically empty of any mention of Lady Dedlock, Esther verges on schizophrenia until the arrival of Inspector Bucket. Bucket's canny pretense of ignorance of the connection between Esther and Lady Dedlock forms the psychic background against which she can join the last effort to bring Lady Dedlock back into community, into life, into the intolerable Confusion of love and dishonor from which the older woman is fleeing, even to her death. Esther goes on with him, in hope, under the strict control of loving duty—which shoves the intolerable into Confusion, to be released in dreams, while it copes consciously with the merely awful, with the snow, the wet, the hurry, the uncertainty, the sight of others in trouble, or the more shattering sight of others untroubled—that the search may continue, the effort to do good stay in action.

This is the saving quality in Esther, not of repression, but of instinctive discipline in the presence of a world/story larger than, though inclusive of, her own: "I had no need to remind myself," she tells us with no narrative flutter of distress, "that I was not there, by the indulgence of any feeling of mine, to increase the difficulties of the search, or to lessen its hopes, or enhance its delays. I remained quiet." This quality wins from Bucket the classic praise of the "pattern" Dickens woman: "a young lady . . . as mild as she's game, and as game as she's mild . . . becomes a Queen." Game women abound—Bucket has his fine appreciation of the murdering, spitting Hortense—and so do mild ones; what churl could fail to love the gentle Ada? But the fusion, the confusion, is indeed Queenly, and Esther is never more so than when she describes with simplicity the end of her search—"I lifted the heavy head, put the long dank hair aside and turned the face. And it was my mother, cold and dead"— and continues her story:

I proceed to other passages of my narrative. From the goodness of all about me, I derived such consolation as I can never think of unmoved. I have already said so much of myself, and so much still remains, that I will not dwell upon my sorrow. I had an illness, but it was not a long one; and I would avoid even this mention of it, if I could quite keep down the recollection of their sympathy.

I proceed to other passages of my narrative.

The chapter which ends her mother's life is followed by a chapter containing an announcement of Ada's pregnancy and Richard's likely death, and titled, with no sentimentality at all, "Perspective." At the price of confusion, with the help of an illness which blurs, in obedience to the drive of *narrative* past the voids of paralyzed feeling, one proceeds. To identify oneself as, to range oneself with, the storytellers, is to lay hands on a great magic for use in the extremities of personal crisis.

III

Esther's kind of storyteller not only has more flexibility in solving or moving beyond her personal crises, she also has greater flexibility of movement in the world of her story. Since her purpose is the full telling of a story larger than herself and her own past to an audience wider than herself and her own present or future, her feats of memory, her insights into other minds, her happy presence at the crucial scenes of so many other lives are more credible than David's or Pip's. For her purpose in the writing is different from theirs. The story that is larger than her own is more real to her, hence has more body than the larger stories in *David Copperfield* and *Great Expectations* have to their narrators. She is "obliged to write all this . . . as if this narrative were the narrative of *my* life!" But it is more than the narrative of her life, and Esther is right to think (and hope) that she will "soon fall into the background now." She does fall back, for she is committed in her narrative not only to materials, lives, events *not* exclusively hers, but also to a reader-listener not exclusively herself.

But she falls into the background less than she expects. She will discover in the telling, with anxiety and wonder, that her material keeps moving in to include herself and her story; she will find in the writing, with amusement and horror, that the reader keeps moving in to become herself. In fact, a whole series of images in *Bleak House* carries through Esther's sense of what a hair-raising, unpredictable, tyrannical experience writing is, and can be, especially for a woman. Caddy Jellyby "stains" herself with ink until she is scarcely distinguishable from one of her splotched pages; ink, like mud and fog, corrodes and mires the world of the novel. Esther's maid Charley finds writing "a trying business" to learn; in her hand "every pen appeared to become perversely animated, and to go wrong and crooked, and to stop, and splash, and sidle into corners." And the bride Esther meets at Chesney Wold whose husband can't write "yet—he's going to learn of me," signs the register with a cross, sharing in public his ignorance until she can share in private her skill. Managing one's writing is an important lesson to learn, and Dickens seems to suggest that one learns it best from the bride's, and Esther's, oblique graces rather than from Mrs. Jellyby's strident, mission-oriented method of attack.

Whatever the lapses into the foreground of the narrative, Esther's first loyalty, according to the narrative conceit in which Dickens was forced to place her—was enabled for once to place an autobiographer because s/he is a woman—is to the large concrete world, which includes herself, and to her unknown friend, the reader, who is also, but not alone, herself. David's and Pip's purpose in the writing, according to Dickens's narrative conceit, is first and last self-reflexive; they write to confess, to discover, to exorcise, apparently, but above all to rekindle emotions and to experience again their lives, the process by which they came to be. David Copperfield especially narrates process from a position of rest; his is a case of rest seeking restlessness again. Pip's purpose, too, is to describe how he came to his present rest, but Dickens's unsettledness as to what that place of rest is—alone, married to Estella with "the shadow of no parting"—suggests that the position of rest is as alien to Dickens's autobiographers as it was to the author himself. In that sense he was truest to his autobiographical voice in *Bleak House,* which is narrated from a position of restlessness and broken off when rest threatens.

David writes to describe the taming of, and to rediscipline, "an undisciplined heart," but narrative truth is evaded time and again by a heart that bursts the discipline of the past tense to evoke like magic a shimmering eternal present-past. Especially in the chapters called "retrospects," chapters startlingly like the present-tense narrative of *Bleak House,* except for the sarcastic bite of the latter, there beats the exhilarated blood of a high heart. Time after time, David went to

Agnes in distress of mind and was made peaceful, drank from that spring and went away again, but his heart, though wise enough now to be astonished at his earlier blindness, was innocent of duplicity: "I write the truth. Whatever contradictions and inconsistencies there were within me, as there are within so many of us; whatever might have been so different, and so much better; whatever I had done, in which I had perversely wandered away from the voice of my own heart; I knew nothing of. I only knew that I was fervently in earnest, when I felt the rest and peace of having Agnes near me." Sincere he was, yet the contradiction remains in the very texture of the narrative; the voice of his heart leads him not only to Agnes but *away* from rest. Exploring this contradiction, following this voice, he writes partly to expose and try again to decipher the great secret: what *is* "that old unhappy feeling . . . like a strain of sorrowful music faintly heard in the night"? But behind this is David's even more important question: who shares that lost, restless, secretly outraged feeling of anticlimax in adult life, that lack of objective correlative to desire and dread? Is it a feeling "general and unavoidable" to the race of man, or is it "particular to me, and might have been different"?

On this question hinges part of the moral authority of autobiography. David doesn't directly answer it, except to indicate that he once balanced between these two notions with "no distinct sense of their opposition" and now considers them "irreconcileable" opposites. The greater authority, I would argue, belongs to an autobiography like *Bleak House,* which does continue to balance these opposites, which renders a particular case with the intensity available only to one who does experience her singularity and who yet remains open to, anxious about, not preachy on, the hints of universality in the case. If the particular and the general are opposites, if the core feeling around which the autobiography closes is perceived as particular to David, then the core feeling, the unhappy feeling, "might have been different" with a better family, and can even now be "cured" when David finds "home" at last with Agnes. And indeed the final page seems to picture a "tranquility" achieved with "a better knowledge of myself" and Agnes. Yet the tranquility is a strange one. The final chapter is another one of those present-tense retrospects which suggest most powerfully the enraptured gaze upon magic faces, magic scenes, which is the crucial narrative conceit of the novel: "In fulfillment of the compact I have made with myself, to reflect my mind on this paper, I again examine it, closely, and bring its secrets to the light." The images which arise in that magic mirror grip with near demonic power, and the author, like Faust, must "subdue" his desire to linger, they are so fair. More striking still, David, in his last paragraph, imagines in the mirror of the future the hard-won "realities" melting from him "like the shadows which I now dismiss." Further, this Prospero pictures Agnes, symbol of tranquility, not joining him in a final Reality but rather "pointing upward," where the restless heart rests at last. Perhaps.

The question of particular and general seems fairly well closed for Pip, whose moral authority, he seems to know, derives exactly from his personal echo of the universal dilemma raised memorably in the lament of the first great criminal-saint autobiographer, Paul of Tarsus—what I would do, that I do not, and what I would not, that I do! Pip's mesmerized gaze into the magic mirror of his mind differs from David's, especially in this bitter understanding: he knew his contradictions, his perversities, his corruptions right from the start. All the secrets were soon out: Joe is worth ten of Estella; the joys given free and clear to him—Biddy's critical regard, Herbert Pocket's loyalty—far outvalue the poisoned promise of Great Expectations. He knew it, but diagnosis is not cure—he behaved as if he did not know it. The past is past, all but one part of it, the bewildered pain of recognition, again, at the gap between knowledge and behavior, between understanding and will, a permanent pain and a universal one, he knows. Why did he behave against his knowledge? "How do I know! Why did you who read this, commit that not dissimilar inconsistency of your own, last year, last month, last week?" Thus Pip is in guilty fellowship with his reader, who has also surely bound himself or herself in "the long chain of iron or gold, of thorns or flowers"—that chain whose decisive link was forged in moral timidity by a heart not alone undisciplined but radically unknown, undefined. "It is the same," says Pip, "with any life," the more so because the condition is not derived from bad models or too early contact with evil (or to be avoided by avoiding these things): "In a word, I was too cowardly to do what I knew to be right, as I had been too cowardly to avoid doing what I knew to be wrong. I had had no intercourse with the world at that time, and I imitated none of its many inhabitants who act in this manner. Quite an untaught genius, I made the discovery of the line of action for myself."

Pip is not, like David, simply talking to his own heart here, not exactly. There is not the constant hypnotized fall into the undiscipline of the present tense, as if the people and the scenes of his past were still in their solid/ghost forms around him. There is an auditor, someone who, to use this book's crucial narrative conceit, is to be handed, over and over, "the clue by which I am to be followed into my poor labyrinth." There is a reader who needs reminding, before *he* falls into mazed contemplation of another's story, that he is seeing his own story. And the reminders are always geared, as are Pip's to himself, to reporting how wide, how nearly impossible to travel or communicate across, is the labyrinth of that gap between understanding and will. "Why repeat it a thousand times?" Pip repeats, "So it always was." The unspoken "so it always will be" hovers over all three of the endings Dickens considered, especially the last two, which, with their rising evening mists showing "tranquil light" on a path out of "the ruined place," seem exactly to parallel the death moment, with restless heart ascending alone, that claims David Copperfield's imagination in his last paragraph. Despite the reader, then, Pip finishes essentially alone; his narrative has been the thousandth trip into the labyrinth, the thousandth gaze into the magic mirror that shows a face alone, and if he had a companion, or an audience, "you who read this," it is one so like himself, so known, as to be little challenge to his bitter look upon himself, just a ghost behind his shoulder in the mirror.

Esther Summerson's reader/friend is unknown; her mother's face is only partly known from beginning to end, "in a confused way, like a broken glass to me." Her own identity is only partly known; even in the first security of Bleak House there remains "an undefinable impression of myself as being something different from what I then was." Confirmation of confusion comes when the smallpox brings first the delirium that makes confusion near dissolution. In her dreams, the identities of child, elder girl, and little woman that she has been trying to unite become separate and strung out; it is impossible to "reconcile them," for they have become "colossal staircases" up which she "labours," forever turned into endless branchings of stairs by obstructions like "a worm in a garden path." And finally, "strung together somewhere in great black space, there was a flaming necklace, or ring, or starry circle of some kind, of which *I* was one of the beads! And . . . my only prayer was to be taken off from the rest, and . . . it was such inexplicable agony and misery to be a part of the dreadful thing."

Is this the nightmare of community and duty, the terrible side of those loving commitments Esther has consciously made? Some read it so. But the proximity of these descriptions to Esther's sense of her multiple selves, and the similarity to Pip's description of his labyrinth, suggest to me rather that Esther is here experiencing the nightmare of solipsism, of being caught in a ring, a staircase, an endless series of receding selves once the gaze is really fixed permanently inward, once the self is fully known as separate from the world. It is, simply, a knowledge better held in Confusion.

That is why there are two, or perhaps three, stages in Esther's recovery from the symbolic fever she experiences at mid-novel. Both have to do with accepting her new face, which is itself a confusion of past and future features. She first becomes aware that she is "something different from what I then was" by way of the absence of mirrors; the loving solicitude (and the loving fear) of her friends has removed them for a time, just as she, in loving solicitude (and fear) removed herself from her friends when she contracted the sickness. By the action of her friends she knows herself both loved and feared, therefore both unchanged and changed. This confusion she accepts, and is able to advance further: she feels the clear imperative to find and fully forgive in advance that changed unchanged face. Standing gamely but mildly before the muslin-veiled mirror at Boythorn's, she doubly veils herself with her own hair. Then she unveils the mirror, the eye of the Other, and finally, unveils herself and looks "at the reflection in the mirror, encouraged by seeing how placidly it look[s] at me." The unknown, who is here *both* the observer and the observed, is bravely and hopefully addressed, and becomes better known: "At first, my face was so strange to me, that I think I should have put my hands before it and started back, but for the encouragement I have mentioned. Very soon it became more familiar, and then I knew the extent of the alteration in it better than I had done at first. It was not like what I had expected; but I had expected nothing definite, and I dare say anything definite would have surprised me."

Dickens's splendid conceit here, that Esther received encouragement from the placid gaze of the unknown face to whom she unveiled her own, is surely the crucial metaphor of this autobiography. For that face is not only hers, it is ours; just as the unknown friend to whom she writes her narrative is not only us but herself as well. Surely it is impossible to address either one's partly known, labyrinthine, undisciplined heart or the reader's without deciding in advance to forgive it, without desiring in advance its forgiveness, and trusting in its love. It is surely this trust in, this desire for, the unknown, or partly known, that allows Esther to expose throughout the narrative, with some continuing trouble, her own unknowing-ness—"I did not know that then, I am not sure that I know it now," she affirms in the last paragraph—to our unknowingness. In this perspective her reluctance to close the narrative definitively—"even supposing———" she says, looking up for our gaze—is even more a tribute to *our* desirability and independence than to her modesty. For we *are* desired. More through this narrator than any other he created in continuing recognition of that "more complicated and passionate relationship with my readers than any writer of my time," Dickens desired his reader in *Bleak House*. And what he desired most of all, like Esther, was that most positive gift, "nothing definite." Among the many symbolic pressures accumulating in the text against closing the narrative, this one was paramount, I think: to leave in operation the mutual current of this desire.

Epitaphic Chapter Titles and the New Mortality of *Bleak House*

Garrett Stewart

> As he spoke thus, with a countenance radiant with joy and triumph, he was withdrawn by those who had brought him into the apartment, and executed within an hour, dying with the same enthusiastic firmness which his whole life had evinced.
>
> Scott, *Old Mortality*

> "My father expected a Judgment," said Miss Flite. "My brother. My sister. They all expected a Judgment. The same that I expect."
> "They are all—"
> "Ye-es. Dead of course, my dear," said she.
>
> Dickens, *Bleak House*

Dickens had begun even by the time of *Dombey and Son* to experiment with those condensed, suggestive chapter headings that become one of the hallmarks of his later fiction, pregnant phrases that often issue in referential twins or triplets. Probably the chapters of *Bleak House* are the most richly titled of all, the progressive umbrellaing of Dickens's rubrics by now in full bloom, and almost every chapter, with the regular exception of those shy, self-effacing ones called "Esther's Narrative," yields a multiple and embracing relevance unfolded as we read. In the epitaphic chapters with which we are primarily concerned, the titles in every case but two take part as stylistic counters in the ambiguous rhetoric of the death scene. At such times the grip of title upon theme does more than simply spread

From *ELH* 45, no. 3 (Fall 1978). © 1978 by the Johns Hopkins University Press.

out like some web-footed, prehensile designation; it may by its am-
bivalence seem to bestride the chasm of mortality itself, both acknowledging the great divide and erecting a bridge across it, through
a taut phrasing that entitles both the temporal and the eternal to
opposite shores of the same disclosed gulf. The best thing about such
duplicitous titles in *Bleak House,* as with "An Appeal Case," is often
not the particular metaphors or ironies of their separate meanings but
the very fact of absolute doubleness, the pun as a sundering of reference that still forces eternity to abut suddenly on time. Like the
contained symbolism of Dickens's death scenes, in other words, the
bracketing titles may also operate as exploratory pivots between
worlds, between discrete spheres of reference.

Miss Barbary dies, for instance, in "A Progress," which therefore comes to signal not only Esther's growth to maturity and her
rise in fortune, but also, in something of Bunyan's sense, a bitter
pilgrimage on Miss Barbary's part that is no more than prolonged
moral stasis, this and also its end. Her ironic "progress" is thus an
unrelieved journey through life and her final step beyond—the mortal egress. This departure is followed five chapters later with the
novel's second death scene in "Covering a Multitude of Sins," on
which implied roster can be listed, within the limits of this single
chapter, the moral slackness and vacillation of Harold Skimpole, the
seductive labyrinth of Jarndyce vs. Jarndyce as explained to Esther
for the first time by her guardian, the inexhaustible coercive charity
of Mrs. Pardiggle, which "begins at home" through the intimidation
of her children into offering weekly donations, the poverty and squa-
lor discovered at the brickmaker's, and finally the matter-of-fact
death there of an unnamed child. It is indeed this last event that
registers a more than either idiomatic or metaphoric claim on the
title. To "cover sins" is in the reportorial sense to provide evils with
blanket coverage; in a satiric second sense it refers to the hypocrisy of
a legal system that masquerades its mercenary lip service to justice as
the real thing, as well as to that related private masking of amorality
in sham empathy and empty good works. But the sin of a child's
death, the social crime which its tiny corpse represents, is in a painfully direct third sense "covered" over, through an act of delicate,
genuine charity, by Esther's handkerchief. The embodied presence in
death of sins that have long been covered up renders the chapter title
poignantly literal, with the typical accoutrement of a sentimental,

tearful death scene in fiction, the lady's fine handkerchief, here transformed instead to the child's covering shroud.

There is of course another, more obvious point to be made about a narrator's obligation to the oblique in the titling of death scenes: that it is first if not foremost a concession to the laws of suspense. To be unambiguously mortuary is to give the narrator's game away even before the character's. Yet the merely inevitable strategies of avoidance are often given double valence in Dickens's chapter titles, part of the abiding logic of his funereal style. The pat expression, the catchy or merely serviceable title abruptly revised by death, the words rotated, for example, to their obverse literal or metaphorical sense—such habitual phrase-spinning exemplifies the double vision of Dickens's death rhetoric. It is one of the strictest axioms of the Dickensian death scene, as we have begun to notice, that eternity, however thinly imagined, hinges on time, fate on temporal works. Dickens does not have to convince us, or himself, that he believes in the Church's doctrinal adjudications, the manifest destinies of heaven or hell, or in any other formulaic immortality, in order to guide his ironies, to empower his symbolic reprisals and dispensations. The specter of a questioned orthodoxy cannot throttle the brilliant thanatology of his greatest passages, where, even without a considered faith in the Christian destiny and its alternate destinations, still the double-faced term "momentous" seems just right for the ambiguous hinging of his imagery. As with Dickens's best titles for such chapters, the "moment" of death in them which the titles so often partly designate is defined by a symbolic fulcrum around which life and fate are pivotally disposed. With Gridley's demise, we are about to see again that rigorous moral leverage by which the living balance, once ironically righted by the equilibrations of Dickens's poetic justice, is instantaneously tipped into eternity, in the narrative past tense from "then" into "thereafter." "What's time," says Mrs. Snagsby, "to eternity?" This stray remark stays in the mind, and chapter titles like "An Appeal Case," among other stylistic devices, give us the ratio she asks about.

Gridley's death follows upon Nemo's in more than chronology, for together they form a diptych of self-destruction. Nemo dies in the grips of his private Banshee, symbolic starvation, an inanition of the spirit that gnaws even through the numbness of opium; Gridley, his rage so long feeding on itself, dies when this spiteful sustenance deserts him. The one man "lived—or didn't live" through his Chancery writing; the other kept alive only through railing against the injustices of the same system. Only in death, the great leveller, is this transparent antithesis seen through. Nemo goes quietly, death in league with a life that approximates it asymptomatically, meeting its limit at infinity. For Nemo death is that slow slippage to epitome. Gridley's life, seemingly by contrast, has been an assertive violence fending against deadness. His death is the opposite, a giving out and a giving up. Narcosis vs. rage, but they both lay waste their victim, coming at last to the same thing: an enervation and an ending.

Speaking of Gridley's imminent demise, the trooper George says: "I seemed to hear the roll of the muffled drums." George euphemizes death by military metaphor, just as two sentences before he used that even more formulaic metaphor of epitome, drawn from his own life rather than Gridley's: "He is on his last march, miss, and has a whim to see her." The trooper envisions death as the last leg of a forced march, a trooping through life, while Gridley has elicited such an epitomizing metaphor earlier out of his own *idée fixe,* saying about the injustices of Chancery: "I will accuse the individual workers of that system against me, face to face, before the great eternal bar!" This is the entirely poetic, non-bureaucratic justice to which death ushers him, yet his hope for a Judgment above, an appeal at last answered by the Appellate Court of eternity, may well be meant to reduce his aspirations to the mad fantasies of Miss Flite, the very comparison which he for so long tried to avoid.

Gridley had once explained to Jarndyce that his monomaniacal railing against the Chancery octopus was not madness so much as a stay against it; it seemed to him all that separated him from his avoided counterpart, Miss Flite, and so he was entrapped by the paradox of a mind-destroying rage used to sustain his wits against idiocy: "There's nothing between doing it, and sinking into the smiling state of the poor little mad woman that haunts the Court." When his own powers have clearly failed him nine chapters later, from nothing of course but futile overuse, his reduced energy removes the distance between himself and Miss Flite, as Esther's tentative phrasing struggles at more than one level to suggest: "Touchingly and awfully drawn together, he and the little mad woman were side by side, and, as it were, alone." What she means by that last phrase is in part, in the words of her next sentence, that "none of us went close to them," but only in part; even when Gridley and Miss Flite share each other's company, their identities have by now so far blended, in his view, as to leave him no second person, "as it were," to define his purposes against. Together at last with Miss Flite (and this is what at least Dickens had partly in mind with the phrase) Gridley is scorchingly "alone," with only his hapless second self to comfort him. Of "all the living and the dead world," Gridley is now forced to acknowledge, "this one poor soul alone comes natural to me." The conjunction incriminates; diction offers circumstantial evidence. With an ambivalent thrift of phrase Dickensian narrative is elsewhere tensed to hold at the margin of death, hold out hope, hold off confirmation, while here it is able to scuttle a disjunction regularly taken for granted between worlds alive and dead. There is not a soul besides Miss Flite waiting for Gridley in death because in effect he has arrived. The phrasing has a way of obviating futurity. With the colluding ambiguity of "soul" (colloquial for person, doctrinal for spirit), the compound phrase subtly expounds a death-in-life for both characters, a purgatorial hinterland in which these two emotional pariahs share, without appeasing, their solitude. Gridley knows he is at one with Miss Flite, but still refuses her blessing:

> The roof rang with a scream from Miss Flite, which still rings in my ears.
> "O no, Gridley!" she cried, as he fell heavily and calmly back before her, "not without my blessing. After so many years!"

Ire has cooled to irony in his death, his one moment of "calm" in the novel, a perverse and involuntary repose. It is also an about-face rather than an epitome that leaves him face to face with his destined identity in the defeated Miss Flite, deaf to her appeal as the court has always been to his. The spiritual "Appeal Case," now before "the great eternal bar," gets no earthly hearing.

The stasis and entropy of Nemo and the self-atrophying fury of Gridley diagnose the same sordid tragedy from opposite but converging perspectives which meet at their mutual vanishing point, the ironic death scene. In fiction, unlike in life, death is never entirely an accident, and Dickens works tirelessly in *Bleak House* to convert authorial providence into psychological or spiritual inevitability. Death is inbred, and the subsequent third death of a character involved in Chancery, that of Krook, is a blatant allegory to this effect. Death for the dead at heart, or the doomed, as with Nemo's guttering candle engendering its own shroud, is merely life unfurling.

Inherent deterioration is what, more than any novelist before him, Dickens had the symbolic powers to explore, demonstrating in his pages that adjusted realism in which death is rarely a discrete, externally derived event but an inward eventuation, a metaphor before and after it is a fact, not contingent so much as spiritually indigenous—the explicative death, like Gridley's or especially Krook's, that needs no naturalistic explanation.

One suspects that this is precisely why Dickens goes to such lengths, in the book itself and its preface, to solicit credence for his metaphor of spontaneous combustion—to suggest that, even as an allegory, it is too true to life. Like the pseudonym Nemo, Krook's name is also more a comment than a denomination. When we first note his curious name painted on a sign above his rag and bottle shop, we are told that the shop is "kept . . . by one Krook"—which we can scarcely avoid hearing as "one crook among many," a synecdoche for the law and its material refuse, of which Krook's junk shop is a travesty. He is even called "the Lord Chancellor" to cement the satire, his shop nicknamed "The Court of Chancery." It is in this very shop, a microcosm of the Chancery at large for which he is a "law-writer," that Nemo, true to his name, lived and/or died. Krook's death follows Nemo's and Gridley's in a chapter whose first sentence conjures shades of the 23rd Psalm for an explicit connection between law and life's surest equity, death itself, when the precincts of the great Court at Lincoln's Inn are called the "perplexed and troublous valley of the shadow of the law."

With three ballistic puns and a final play on legalistic terminology (my italics), Dickens wrote in the last paragraph of the opening chapter: "A *battery* of blue bags is *loaded* with heavy *charges* of papers and carried off by clerks; the little mad old woman marches off with her documents; the empty court is locked up. If all the injustice it has committed, and all the misery it has caused, could only be locked up with it, and the whole burnt away in a great funeral pyre,—why so much the better for other *parties* than the *parties* in Jarndyce and Jarndyce!" When the symbolic charge so loaded is suddenly detonated later in the novel and "one Krook" goes up in the smoke of his own instantaneous pyre, this cremation from within is recorded as an epitome of his nickname as well as his nature: "The Lord Chancellor of that Court, true to his title in his last act, has died the death of all Lord Chancellors in all Courts, and of all authorities in all places under all names soever, where false pretenses are made, and where injustice is done. Call the death by any name Your Highness will, . . . it is the same death eternally—inborn, inbred, engendered in the corrupted humours of the vicious body itself, and that only—Spontaneous Combustion, and none other of all the deaths that can be died." The play on "body" for the locus of organic corruption and the body politic at large completes the microcosmic irony.

As with Nemo's death in the same house, again the genius of the scene lies in the mobile ironies of the chapter title, "The Appointed Time," and the necrological decor of its setting. Weevle explains the strangely designated hour at which Krook will turn over Nemo's papers as if some fate beyond Krook's ken or control were directing the man's perverse whims: "What does he do anything for? *He* don't know. Said, to-day was his birthday, and he'd hand 'em over to-night at twelve o'clock." Patterning like this has its designs upon us. Death is somehow to be threaded back upon birth. Weevle has earlier that night heard Krook singing "the only song he knows—about Bibo, and old Charon, and Bibo being drunk when he died, or something or other." It is the perfect birthday hymn for a man who dies of drink (condition transferred to cause) before the time he himself has appointed, at the exact last minute of his sacred day, for an illegal transaction. Just as his birthday is about to run out, his existence goes with it, his symbolic lifeline knotted off like an umbilical cord. At a party later for Mrs. Bagnet, Mr. George apologizes for discussing Jo's death in the middle of the festivities, "for it's not birthday talk." Yet in the deepest allegorical sense with Krook, to die on the day of his birth, even the commemorative anniversary of that day, is never to have lived, which is what suicidal lives like Krook's or Nemo's look like to Dickens.

But Krook's death is more than the foregone conclusion of his own story, for it also serves as the displaced crisis and climax of Esther Summerson's. Jo the crossing-sweeper is society's victim, Esther its martyr. Jo, stricken with the fever society fosters in its squalid orphans, carries it to Bleak House, where it is passed from servant to mistress, Charley to Esther, in a hierarchy of retribution against the least guilty—an undeserved vengeance that scars, temporarily blinds, and nearly destroys Esther. Yet between the time when Esther contracts the fever and is blinded by it and the description of her gradual recovery, as if in symbolic reprisal for society's own blindness and neglect, the novel's plot is concerned primarily with the death of Krook, a namesake for the Court whose corrupt evasions are symptomatic of society's indifference to the plight and the "appeals" of the citizens it is supposed to serve. When we return after this three-chapter interval to "Esther's Narrative," Krook has in some sense already died for her, the Lord Chancellor for the sins and insidious infections of his parodic realm. Sequence is consequence in Dickensian narrative, the order of events as well as their individual import, symbolic. Society's inborn corruption has momentarily consumed itself in the person of its own "vicious body," and the innocent scapegoat, Esther, can be released from sacrifice and renewed.

During her fever, one of Esther's hallucinatory visions stands as a surrealistic parable of willed escape—from life or from dying, from herself or her niche in society, such are the ambiguities of the image: "Dare I hint at that worst time when, strung together somewhere in great black space, there was a flaming necklace, or ring, or starry circle of some kind, of which *I* was one of the beads! And when my only prayer was to be taken off from the rest, and when it was such inexplicable agony and misery to be a part of the dreadful thing?" This is life, the interconnectedness of life in the social fabric, but it is also, and in desperate particular for Esther, the aristocratic nexus which she has begun, in her observed resemblance to Lady Dedlock, to suspect her part in. Soon after the death of her unknown father Nemo, much earlier in the book, there is a description of Chesney Wold which is perhaps being adverted to with the hallucinatory symbol of Esther's demonic necklace: "Seen by night, from distant openings in the trees, the row of windows in the long drawing-room, where my Lady's picture hangs over the great chimney piece, is like a row of jewels set in a black frame." It is exactly from the resemblance to Lady Dedlock that Esther will soon wish herself delivered in her fever, a likeness Guppy has detected when standing before this very portrait. There is a sense, then, in which this feverish wish for escape comes true in the very disfigurement which destroys the resemblance like a reflection in a shattered mirror. With an image which again connects her ordeal forward to Jo's death, Esther also recalls how in her feverish visions she "laboured up colossal staircases, ever striving to reach the top, and ever turned, as I have seen a worm in a garden path, by some obstruction, and labouring again . . . 'O more of these never-ending stairs, Charley—more and more—piled up to the sky, I think!' " The double-edged symbol tells, it would seem, of her heroic effort to keep life marginally underway, and at the same time offers an image of death ambiguously struggled toward, the spirit heavenward tending but always turned aside. Just before life climbs painfully, inch by inch, to oblivion, death and the wished-for release are indistinguishable.

This is a febrile limbo from which Esther returns, deflected and brought back from the final dark at the top of the stairs—and from the greater light, as Jo's death not altogether ironically implies, just past it. When a metaphor similar to Esther's staircase reappears at Jo's death scene, the homeless boy does stumble up the final step and across the threshold: "For the cart so hard to draw, is near its journey's end, and drags over stony ground. All round the clock it labours up the broken steps, shattered and worn. Not many times can the sun rise, and behold it still upon its weary road." The metaphor of the cart is originally sprung from an accidental pun of the illiterate boy's, prodded further by one of the narrator's on "death rattle": "Allan Woodcourt lays his hand upon his pulse, and on his chest. 'Draw breath, Jo!' 'It draws,' says Jo, 'as heavy as a cart.' He might add, 'and rattles like it'; but he only mutters, 'I'm a moving on, sir.' " This character who has led a life of slavish manual labor, this itinerant crossing-sweeper repeatedly swept on and away by others, knows the phrase "drawing breath," the essence of mortal sustenance, only by analogy with the physical labor of drawing a cart, and imagines dying, in such terms, as a last clattering haul, explicitly as that ultimate "moving on" by which society has repeatedly hoped to rid its sight of him. "Moving on" has been raised exponentially again, like so many catch phrases in Dickens, to an instantaneously coined Victorian euphemism equivalent to "passing on." It becomes a painfully vivid instance of death as an "absolutizing" (Burke's term)—or an epitomization—of life's determining logic, mortality as the ultimate Vagrancy. Such a metaphor for death as one last dose of life consorts direly with the initial description of the boy's neighborhood, which exposes in the idiomatic verb "live" (for "dwell"), given the nature of his sordid existence, a thoughtless misnomer: "Jo lives—that is to say, Jo has not yet died—in a ruinous place."

Earlier we have heard, in an authorial apostrophe to the boy, that "the be-all and end-all of your strange existence upon earth" is "Move on! You are by no means to move off, Jo, for the great lights can't at all agree about that. Move on!" There is no escape permitted, only a beating time until the "be-all" becomes epitomized in the "end-all" and the only place on earth to move on to is off at last.

Nearer this point of no return, Esther encounters the boy at Jenny's cottage. Jo, feverish, says "I'm a going somewheres," and when Esther asks Jenny where, Jo answers for himself: "Somewheres . . . I have been moved on, and moved on, more nor ever I was afore. . . . And I'm a-going somewheres. That's where I'm a-going." Esther now asks Jenny what they can do for him, and the sad old woman replies with a kind of agnostic reverence: "I know no more, ma'am, than the dead. . . . Perhaps the dead know better, if they could only tell us." A few pages later the boy disappears, afraid that Esther, as her look-alike and mother had done once before, would make him go to the "berryin' ground." Esther hears from one of the servants at Bleak House that he has fled:

> "It's the boy, miss," said he.
> "Is he worse?" I inquired.
> "Gone, miss."
> "Dead!"
> "Dead, miss? No. Gone clean off."

Esther, perhaps recalling the boy's own obsession with "going somewheres," mistakes literal truth for euphemism, while in fleeing from his one chance for care and recuperation, Jo has indeed "moved on" toward his last release. He has half-knowingly tried to do what the servant's explanation, "gone clean off," at first implied, as echoed shortly by Skimpole's opinion that "he had, with great natural politeness, taken himself off." To move on until you move off once and for all is the climaxing of be-all and end-all which happens metaphorically when we find Jo at his final spatial impasse, dying in Mr. George's gallery.

Since Dickens had already used "Moving On" as a chapter title, he finds for Jo's exit chapter, instead of this injunction turned metaphor and epitome, the even more richly ambiguous "Jo's Will." He has repeatedly expressed his desire for escape, his will to pass away, in the single-word, pre-Joycean sentence "Wishermaydie." He has also asked near the end, willed, that an apology be written for his having brought the fever to Bleak House, a document which would thus become in a third sense his last will and testament, the only legacy he can bequeath—not the kind of monetary remembrance subject to Chancery litigation, but a heartfelt apology, above and beyond secular law, for the ironies of fate and mortality. The remaining request of this last will is that he be "laid along with"

Nemo, his one friend in life and his surrogate father, a man who is also the natural parent of Esther herself. Esther has, because of Jo's contagion, narrowly missed such a reunion with her dead source, yet it is all Jo has to look forward to.

It is this theme of the rejoined father with which the prayer Jo is taught at his death so unashamedly, though not unironically, resonates. Even the doctor who prescribes and administers this spiritual medicine has been present at the deathbed of the boy's surrogate earthly father, for Allan Woodcourt (called "Woodcot" by Jo in another unintended pun, perhaps in a Ruskinian moment of unconscious pastoral itch on the part of this street urchin) "softly seats himself upon the bedside with his face towards him—just as he sat in the law writer's room—and touches his chest and heart. The cart had nearly given up, but labours on a little more." The death scene provides the culmination of the cart journey as an emblem of life's trek, replacing it with that motif of illumination set over against spiritual benightedness which appears later at Richard Carstone's death. The climax of the scene, beginning here with Jo's burial plea to Woodcourt, is too powerfully compact to abridge. Though the narrative now partially inhabits the allegory of this aimless urban pilgrimage, life as an uphill journey more and more exhausting as it nears its end, still it is poised between an implied external metaphor of diagnosis and the internal, perhaps feverish vision of the dying mind itself.

> "Ah! P'raps they wouldn't do it if I wos to go myself. But will you promise to have me took there, sir, and laid along with him?"
>
> "I will, indeed."
>
> "Thank'ee sir. Thank'ee sir. They'll have to get the key of the gate afore they can take me in, for it's allus locked. And there's a step there, as I used for to clean with my broom,—It's turned very dark, sir. Is there any light a-coming?"
>
> "It is coming fast, Jo."
>
> Fast. The cart is shaken all to pieces, and the rugged road is very near its end.
>
> "Jo, my poor fellow!"
>
> "I hear you, sir, in the dark, but I'm a-gropin—a-gropin—let me catch hold of your hand."

> "Jo, can you say what I say?"
> "I'll say anythink as you say, sir, for I knows it's good."
> "OUR FATHER."
> "Our Father!—yes, that's wery good, sir."
> "WHICH ART IN HEAVEN."
> "Art in Heaven—is the light a-comin, sir?"

The shift in capitalization between text and response may suggest that Jo is in some way domesticating the prayer. The sound of "FA-THER" of course he likes, but "HEAVEN" is too new an idea for any reaction but the ambiguous non sequitur about the awaited lamp—or unknown source of light.

> "Art in Heaven—is the light a-comin, sir?"
> "It is close at hand. HALLOWED BE THY NAME!"
> "Hallowed be—thy—"
> The light is come upon the dark benighted way. Dead!

Death literalizes; the allegory of the cart and the light gives way to the stark fact of mortality, rendered in the past tense as a fatal *fait accompli*.

Jo has learned nothing of God or of Heaven, a fact explicitly charged to the disastrous failures of self-righteous evangelicism, especially to the unilluminated mouthings about "the light of Terewth" by Reverend Chadband, a light that "is come upon" Jo's path only in death. Jo does have some notion of what a father might be, though he has never known any but Nemo. Paternity, the one idea that directly moves him in "The Lord's Prayer," is thus an emblematic type of divinity in this scene. Jo prays, that is, to the abstraction of fatherhood and dies just before repeating the word "name" in this first and last catechism. The name is God, which he does not know, and the truncated last words thus remind us both of this ignorance and of that nameless protector, one Nemo, he knew in life.

The actual lines of the Lord's prayer, just before Jo's death cuts off Allan's recital, would have been, "THY KINGDOM COME, THY WILL BE DONE, ON EARTH AS IT IS IN HEAVEN." In this novel of balked, delusory Judgment, whose chief teleologist is the demented Miss Flite, all glances at apocalypse are, like the Jellyby and Pardiggle philanthropy, too "telescopic." The reign of destruction is in fact upon the earthly city as the novel opens, but no end is in view, no greater City or Kingdom to come. One waits only for the private coming to judgment, the individual submission to the will of eternity. Jo's "Wishermaydie" and his last written testament of remorse yield to the greater Will of destiny and to the light which floods his emergence from the valley of the shadow—or, less religiously, which stands as a mere metaphor for that human end. The questions raised about the ironies that riddle Jo's death scene and divulge its satiric intent tend, I think, to congregate around this arrival of light, phrased so as to parallel the unspoken "thy kingdom come" of the Lord's Prayer: "The light is come. . . ." Is this meant to signal instantaneous access to a kingdom of heaven still removed from earth, but inviting earth's homeless ones to revelation and a final rest? Does death issue the spirit to light, that is, or does death simply constitute light as a figurative antithesis to life, the end of a foul benighted struggle?

Darkness is the opposite of creation's "Fiat lux," and so it finds its way repeatedly into the figuration of death as evidence of the void. When Nemo is discovered, "the candle which has drooped so long, goes out, and leaves him in the dark," the old night of death. Gridley too exits from a stage carefully lit, as will Tulkinghorn, Lady Dedlock, and Richard Carstone later. Gridley has himself been described in a visual metaphor as the "faintest shadow of an object full of form and color," and the sun which at the beginning of his death scene was pictured as "low—near setting" has vanished altogether with his death, the passing of his own shadow and the shadow of Chancery that has so long darkened his way: "The sun was down, the light had gradually stolen from the roof, and the shadow had crept upward." The only ascent is of darkness, the risen and freed shadow of his death-in-life on earth. But is the announced flood of light at Jo's death necessarily the opposite of this? Certainly there is nothing like the narrator's access of confidence at the close of *The Death of Ivan Ilych:* "In place of death there was light." In Dickens light does not displace death so much as rename it. When someone near the dying Ilych utters, knowingly or not, the biblical "It is finished," thinking that the hero's last ordeal, and with it his life, had come to an end, Ilych translates Christ's last words "in his soul" to mean "Death is finished. . . . It is no more!" The great Western novelist perhaps farthest of all from Dickens in his verbal persuasion, the least inclined to word play, however serious, has managed exquisitely to make the pronoun in "It is finished" a pun turning about the most absolute of oppositions and revealed by the double take of the presumed corpse himself. No, Ilych says to himself—not to the living, who could neither hear nor understand—death, not life, is finished, life is just begun.

Part of the difference between agnostic and Christian death scenes is the understanding of the prepositional phrase, whether explicit or merely implied, "in death." In the moment of death? In a subsequent eternity called death? And even when the first interpretation is made, is it a moment that then succeeds to eternal life, or simply, as Jo's death at least partly implies, a first and last instant of blessedness only by contrast with what has gone before? For Ivan Ilych, for Tolstoy at this late point in his career, death comes and goes, and life in a higher key remains, where light replaces death. This is religion for Tolstoy, not inhabited fantasy; it is what both he and his character know to be true. Dickens for the most part owns to his uncertainty, and his picturing of transcendence is a more subjective and ambiguous gambit of language itself, a first verbal move into the unseen. Since it is only through language that the narrator can mediate between temporal sequence and unseen succession, the light we "see" at Jo's death has no more mimetic status than the "cart" we have been watching struggle toward this border of illumination. They are both metaphors, the one generated from Jo's own half-conscious simile, the second too ambiguous to gauge. With rare exception in his novels, Dickens pulls up short of his dying characters in their glimpses of eternity. Dickens cannot be sure that the moment of death is ever "finished," and even if he wishes to treat it as only the penultimate fact of life, a threshold to afterlife, his prose holds at the boundary, where words have something tangible they can confidently affix themselves to, concentrating on death as life's worldly absolutizing rather than its possible divine absolution. Jo is unarguably rewarded, but it may be simply by death itself. "The light is come upon the dark benighted way. Dead!" If the end of a painful blindness is easing light, then death, regardless of its aftermath, can be seen metaphorically as such a light, the only "light of Terewth" at last. It is a manner of speaking, and Jo may have no sense of it whatever. Dickens is never more the acknowledged stylist than in his death scenes. I mean this not only in terms of the agility or gentle equivocation of his evasive genius, but epistemologically. For language, human speech, must always imply its own terminus ad quem; if metaphors are made good when "death is finished," it is beyond the power of metaphors to prove, and verbalization must rest its case.

"Jo's Will" as a title, compacted as it is of good will, death wish, and written legacy of expiation, gives way to "Closing In," the chapter on Tulkinghorn's death. The title refers both to his inexorable approach to a public denunciation of Lady Dedlock and also, by ironic reversal, to the retributive closing in upon him of his own fate, its foreclosure on his mortality. Time will be up for her when he closes in, and for Tulkinghorn himself when eternity descends upon him from the other direction. Allegorically in Dickens, with respect to human feeling, dearth is death, and Tulkinghorn's physical death at the end of a breathing demise also illustrates Dickens's reciprocal mor(t)ality in its narrative timing. Just as Krook's spontaneous combustion follows upon the worst crisis of Esther's fever as an extension of the private ordeal into the symbolic range of the book's social satire, so Jo's death is revenged in the subsequent chapter by the murder of Tulkinghorn. Krook's last chapter was called "The Appointed Time," catching very much the kind of temporal irony that also attends Tulkinghorn's death. Just before the lawyer returns to his chambers on the fatal night, we hear him "muttering reproof to his watch" for its being two minutes wrong: "At this rate you won't last my time." There is not much of it left, and the irony is only intensified if we remember at this point the other of Tulkinghorn's macabre alter egos (besides Nemo, as we will soon see) and that man's earlier gold watch, the "one bachelor friend of his, a man of the same mould and a lawyer too, who lived the same kind of life until he was seventy-five years old, and then, suddenly conceiving (as it is supposed) an impression that it was too monotonous, gave his gold watch to his hairdresser one summer evening, and walked leisurely home to the Temple, and hanged himself." But from such prophetic parables Tulkinghorn himself can learn nothing.

The emotionally heartless Tulkinghorn dies of a bullet through the heart, an organ which has long become for him, in any but a strict anatomical sense, vestigial. The manner in which death will essentialize Tulkinghorn was first prophesied in the novel's second chapter: "There are noble Mausoleums rooted for centuries in retired glades of parks, among the growing timber and the fern, which perhaps hold fewer noble secrets than walk abroad among men, shut up in the breast of Mr. Tulkinghorn." He is a living tomb, and even everyday salutations are among the human currency he "buries . . .

along with the rest of his knowledge." The parasitic inwardness of lawyers is repeatedly stressed in *Bleak House,* from the vulturous Vholes, whose name also suggests vortex and hole, to Tulkinghorn, whose private interior is comprised entirely of the secret inner lives of others, without which entombed privacies he himself would be a hole or void. His is a living silence unto death, and negation is the essence of his public self, for at the beginning of his last chapter we catch him in a characteristic pose devoid of self-projection: "Mr. Tulkinghorn says nothing, looks nothing." A few pages later and the *reductio* has been achieved: is nothing.

And No One. Tulkinghorn learns nothing about himself, it seems, from his seventy-five year old doppelgänger with the gold watch and the suicidal finish, but he has had another alter ego in Nemo the law-writer, instrument at once and fulfilment of Tulkinghorn the lawyer, whose corpse does seem to cause his superior an all too momentary shock of recognition. The man who was the first to realize what "Nemo" meant comes upon the corpse of this nobody and lets blurt his only overt expression of emotion in the novel, the (in his mouth) blasphemous explosion: "God save us! . . . He is dead." If this is more than a figure of speech in first person plural, it implicates Tulkinghorn himself, and all those who have neglected Nemo, in his emaciated demise. But there is also the strong suggestion that in Nemo's starved, spiritually evacuated remains, Tulkinghorn may recognize, unconsciously no doubt, that he is coming face to face, its eyes open and glassily staring, with the No One at his own core, the terrible emptiness of the void. It is a glimpse into what Robert Martin Adams has trenchantly called, in the context of modern nihilism, "the oval mirror of the zero sign." Tulkinghorn does not look long.

The one mystery this ambulatory tomb of secrets never attempted to solve was the meaning of Allegory painted upon the ceiling of his chambers in town, and it hovers over his corpse as "a paralysed dumb witness," in both the everyday and the legal sense, to the murder. To turn verdict and sentence against the lawyer himself is a peripety at least as old as the plays of Shakespeare, Dickens's greatest mentor in the ironic language of mortality, for Hamlet himself detects a graveyard epitome in the supposed skull of a lawyer: "Is this the fine of his fines, and the recovery of his recoveries, to have his fine pate full of fine dirt?" (*Hamlet,* 5, 1). The legal term "fine" is cousin to the Latin "finis" and the obsolete form "fine" for "end," so that finality is even verbally latent in the day-to-day professional transactions of a lawyer. So too, in Dickens, with the immediate habitat of Tulkinghorn as a projection of his being and a prediction of its end. As with the wild waves in *Dombey and Son,* what allegory was always bearing "witness" to, warning of, was simply Death itself.

After the shattering sound of the gunshot which we may guess has killed Tulkinghorn, the narrator asks rhetorically: "Has Mr. Tulkinghorn been disturbed? It must be something unusual indeed to bring him out of his shell. . . . What power of cannon might it take to shake that rusty old man out of his immovable composure?" Whatever we have surmised at this point about the loud retort that breaks the stillness of the night, the last question makes perfect sense when asked of the living man or the dead. This spiritually vacated, intractable, almost fossilized creature has all along been entirely "shell," his body its own casket well in advance of his corporeal death. And of course Tulkinghorn is killed by a shell or bullet which, in the spiritual terms mocked by his death, drives what soul there is from the body and leaves it—what in his case it has always been—the empty cartridge of a human being. Death is an optimizing of life, an allegorical compendium as well as an end, the *speculum mortis* held up as a final reflection of life to the audience rather than to the dying consciousness. Lady Dedlock's terror of the man even after his murder goes to the heart of this issue in Dickens, for "from this pursuer, living or dead—obdurate and imperturbable before her in his well-remembered shape, or not more obdurate and imperturbable in his coffin-bed,—there is no escape but in death." The ponderous, stolid repetition imitates and confirms the continuity of Tulkinghorn's death with his so-called life.

This "escape . . . in death" is the refuge Lady Dedlock seeks, from Tulkinghorn himself and from the private guilt he had threatened to publicize. So far from her high station does she flee that, to throw detective Bucket off the track, she has even changed clothes with "Jenny, the mother of the dead child," that beggarly wife of the brickmaker. She has also struggled to an ugly rest at the burial yard in Tom-all-Alone's in an effort to lie at last beside her former lover, if only in death. The whole search after Lady Dedlock becomes for Esther disorienting and hallucinatory—and finally symbolic, as she unwittingly explains in the preceding chapter: "If I ever thought of the time I had been out, it presented itself as an indefinite period of great duration; and I seemed in a strange way never to have been free from the anxiety under which I then laboured." Indeed she has been searching all her life for a mother, for that filial affection so long dead to her. The result has been her own diminished sense of self, her marginal existence, as climaxed in her near-annihilating bout with fever, so that it is scarcely accidental when the warping and elongation of time during this last phase of her search for a mother should be described in terms which reverse her feverish confusions about the duration of her life: "I had never known before how short life really was, and into how small a space the mind could put it." Nor is it accidental that her tracking down of her mother should lead her to the place where most orphans, like Philip Pirrip in *Great Expectations,* discover their origins: at the common graveyard of mother and father, here the pestilent burial heaps at Tom-all-Alone's.

Repeatedly described as "bored to death," and, at the sight of Nemo's handwriting, succumbing to a shock "like the faintness of death," Lady Dedlock appropriately meets her actual death as the epitome of a life long ago abdicated. And so again, as with most characters in this vein of Dickensian narrative, we are presented with no dramatic moment of death, only an *ex post facto* corpse. It runs in the family, for there was no death moment for the novel's first terminal case, either, Lady Dedlock's sister Miss Barbary, who simply prolonged her rigidity across an invisible border, without a word of forethought or farewell. Lady Dedlock's lover also left life in solitude and in silence, "found dead" as Tulkinghorn says—and as he himself as well as Krook will later be. Lady Dedlock too has only her suicidal self, and perhaps her own Banshee of starvation, to assist her out of this world, and no dying words to memorialize her at her point of departure. Private verbalization at such times is a privilege in Dickens, a relaxation of the satirist's rigor. Almost in every case villains are denied immediate last words because they are denied by their very natures the last rights to humanizing self-awareness, the last rites of its expression. Lady Dedlock's end, however, falls halfway between the sympathetic, tragic pole of narrated death, complete with quoted last words as a testament of the expiring will, as in the case of Jo or even Gridley, and the opposite satiric pole of offstage death as a foregone conclusion, for she is allowed some transcribed last words in those letters that come into Bucket's possession. In one of these scrawled notes she explains the deflected suicidal motives which finally align her with Nemo's "accidental" death: "I have no purpose but to die. When I left I had a worse; but I am saved from adding that guilt to the rest. Cold, wet, and fatigue, are sufficient causes for my being found dead; but I shall die of others, though I suffer from these." Her guilt is of course not so much over her illegitimate child as over the emotional suicide of her marriage to Sir Leicester, her perversion of wedlock into deadlock. One suicide per life is enough. Instead her slow death from indolent indifference to her own person, out of station in a lowly disguise as she has always been masked and emotionally misplaced in high society, and still separated from her lover by an iron gate erected by society, is more than direct suicide a fitting epitome.

Edward W. Said has speculated recently about *Beginnings* and about the novel's peculiar place in the enterprise of initiation. The psychology of Esther Summerson, though Said doesn't mention her, exemplifies with admirable compactness what he sees as the "seemingly limitless hovering between nullity and existence that is central to the novelistic conception of character and to its representation in language." Pip in *Great Expectations* is Said's chief example, a character who searches for authority, for autonomy, amid a web of receding and self-implicating filiations. "The basic scheme I have been describing is the cycle of birth and death," Said recapitulates at one point. "Pip's origin as a novelistic character is rooted in the death of his parents. By his wish to make up for that long series of graves and tombstones he creates a way for himself." For Esther, who has as many parental surrogates as Pip can boast in his novel, whether father/benefactors or mother/godmothers, personal identity must also be anchored by origins. Pip is symbolically born in the opening paragraphs of *Great Expectations* out of initiating fantasies about his parents, as inspired by their tombstones, but Esther is denied even these rooting impressions, for very early in *Bleak House* she tells us that "I had never been shown my mama's grave. I had never been told where it was." Esther's genealogical groping takes her back, ultimately, past her discovered mother, Lady Dedlock, and her unknown father, to the Dedlock ghost, whom Esther herself seems in her own eyes to reincarnate as an avenging shame upon the house of Dedlock. But her mother dies for the daughter as Krook in a more purely schematic way had done earlier, Lady Dedlock becoming in Guster's words "lame, and miserable" like the original lamed wife of Sir Morbury, thus (to borrow the words of Nemo's death) establishing her own pretensions to the role and becoming a ghost indeed.

Picking up the text at the unforgettable moment when Esther unknowingly comes upon this corpse-as-epitome, a recognition scene so protracted that it is as if we are watching the mother die before the very eyes of the daughter, we read: "I saw before me, lying on the step, the mother of the dead child." No ambiguity in the novel is so devastatingly fit. The fever that had originally brought the street infection up the social ladder as far as Bleak House was carried by Jo from Tom-all-Alone's to Esther through her servant Charley, and this hierarchy is reversed in the descent by disguise of Lady Dedlock to Tom-all-Alone's, who in her two visits to Jo's environs comes dressed first as her own servant, and then as the indigent and ragged wife of the brickmaker whose child Esther had watched die fifty-one chapters before. She is doing penance for her station's sins of omission against the lower orders. In the clothes of high society's ultimate victim, a desperate pauper, she has become, like her daughter before her during her fever, its scapegoat. And yet Lady Dedlock is in one sense not only mistaken for, she *is,* the mother of a child until now dead.

Esther has held her place among the living weakly indeed, a faltering clutch upon existence like the elided lifelines Geoffrey Hartman discusses, partly because she could claim only a self unacknowledged by its source. After the disfiguring fever, even that tentative former self is mourned as dead: "I felt for my old self as the dead may feel if they ever revisit these scenes. I was glad to be tenderly remembered, to be gently pitied, not to be quite forgotten." Esther becomes not only the avenging Dedlock spector but the Summerson ghost. It is one of the novel's bleakest psychic economies that this girl who once, having never seen her mother's face or her mother's grave, felt scarcely alive, can finally assume her identity only by fulfilling both conditions at once, over the corpse of a mother it is no longer a shame to acknowledge and be seen with. The chief business of the narrative in the chapters immediately following the death scene of Lady Dedlock becomes the gradual revision of Esther's marital plans. Instead of insisting on her promised hand, the middle-aged Jarndyce hands Esther over to her true lover Allan Woodcourt. "I am your guardian and your father, now," he says, admitting to the most he could ever have been. Not forced to marry her father, Esther, unlike Oedipus in Hartman's terms, is finally allowed a lifeline of her own, yet it comes to her only after the long-standing lie about the other half of her parentage has been brought symbolically true before the grave of her original father, Nemo; as Esther had always been led to believe, her mother does die in childbirth—in order to bring the daughter, for the first time safely and securely, into the world. In the instant of its recognition by us, the searing irony of that phrase "the mother of the dead child" is rescinded, cancelled by a reciprocal and appeasing death, and the long dead child has room for once to breathe.

We read on in this scene of post-mortem recognition: "I lifted the heavy head, put the long dank hair aside, and turned the face. And it was my mother, cold and dead." A single metaphoric phrase like "stone cold dead" would not have served. And read from right to left, "dead and cold," as against "dead yet still warm," would have had only a clinical precision to recommend it. The genius of "cold and dead" rests with the blended metaphorical status of both adjectives, seeming at the same time incremental and reversible. Cold as always, she is cold once more and forever, an iciness of spirit declined to absolute zero. Almost imperceptibly, the compound adjectives rephrase essence as cessation, or vice versa, a dead metaphor from life ("cold") and the adjective of termination ("dead") fronting at once upon each other and upon redundancy. The half metaphoric, half literal entwining, the virtual twinning, of "cold and dead" takes on the proportions of a paradigm not only for death scenes in Dickens but for fictional dying at large. Death becomes a subset of life in fiction, and must, since it cannot for the most part be arbitrary, shoulder the burden of a certain redundancy. Like endings generally, death cannot afford to take us by surprise in novels; characters usually lie in wait for *it*. Only if what happens in the last throes of a given characterization is predicated on, and to some extent predictable from, life, can its import have resonance. This is the paradox of climax in the biographical curve of any plot. Only when death is redundant can death's *meaning* have had adequate time to unfold. In an ironic novel such as *Bleak House,* a death scene like Lady Dedlock's must be superfluous and fitting at once, portrayed both as a continuation from life (her end was no better than the rest of her) and a synonym for it (never really alive, she is at last technically dead). Epic or romance may view death under the aspect of heroic life, as in Scott; tragedy or satire, at least the Dickensian crossbreed, tends to view life under the aspect of death. A phrase like "cold and dead" merely makes explicit, and hence more potently redundant, the two terms. Long cold and now dead, she had all along lived—emotionally ended—as she would one day die.

In talking about the human ingredients of plot, E. M. Forster notes that birth and death are "strange because they are at the same time experiences and not experiences. We only know of them by report. . . . Our final experience, like our first, is conjectural. We move between two darknesses." Edward Said goes beyond Forster, for whom life and death transpire in the unlit wings of life's brief hour upon the stage, to suggest that initiations are themselves generated against the threat both of ends and of the anterior void, and that any theory of origination must therefore be intimate with a myth of death. In Said's theory the antinomy of beginning is not end but death, the nullity at *either* end. "The novelistic character gains his fictional authority . . . in the desire to escape death," to enter upon life out of its antedating darkness and to push against the same negation gaining on the self from the other direction. Thus "the narrative process endures so long as that essentially procreative will persists." This is the novelist's will, of course, on behalf of his characters—directly so for the chief protagonist if it is a first-person narrative, as *Bleak House* is by turns. Since, according to Said, "a character's real beginning takes place in the avoidance of the anonymity of pure negation," Hawdon's self-cancelling "rebirth" as Nemo is not only a symbolic suicide but an antitype for Said's theory of fictional generation, the case of a man who wills upon himself his effacement as a man and his erasure as a novelistic character. But by giving up his originating thrust away from death, the animus against nullity that alone is fictionally animating, Nemo also negates one coordinate of origin for Esther, and the matter is dramatically complicated by the failures of the "procreative will" across, as it were, a gap of generation.

In exploring the connection between ends human and fictional in the closing chapter of *The City of Dickens,* Alexander Welsh quotes Forster on one half of the question: "If it was not for death and marriage, I do not know how the average novelist would conclude. Death and marriage are almost his only connection between his characters and his plot." But what about the connection between death itself and marriage? Revising Alan Friedman's notion of these two human rites of passage as alternative "end-stopping" formulas in fiction, Welsh argues instead that, in the traditional novels which Dickens's art exemplifies, endings tend to "superimpose death and marriage," to insinuate the latter, in its narrowing, convergence, and finality of plot, as a metaphor for or anticipation of the former. Welsh thus reads marriages *sub specie mortis* as psychological closures analogous to and prefigurative of death, remarking that: "Narrative endings, whether superficially happy or unhappy, exploited what comfort there is in the stoppage of time." The final death scene in *Bleak House,* Richard Carstone's in "Beginning the World," becomes perhaps the ultimate test case in Dickens for Welsh's sense of death wedded to matrimony, not to mention its ironic reworking of Said's point about beginnings born of ends. Dickens's novels must domesticate eternity, make evident the invisible, along the analogical edge of their glinting language, whether in linguistic quibbles or sustained conceits like the initiation motif in this chapter, with its bipolar title. Not only does Richard die in a subjective confusion between exit and entrance, extinction and second chance, with an accompanying overlap between death and marriage, but his death is followed at once, just pages from the end of the novel, by the sudden exit to silence (by her and about her) of crazed Miss Flite. The question seems raised here just short of explicitly by Dickens: how deeply is death implicated as a matter of course in a narrator's last words about a character? The answer must wait, however, for the death scene that precedes it and lends it occasion.

In discussing those novelistic endings which in his view variously exploit the "stoppage of time," Welsh draws a distinction which Richard's death at least temporarily—and metaphorically—withdraws: "If it were not for their generally peaceful character, such endings might be portrayed well enough by Kermode's model of the apocalypse. But in the period we have been studying the more obvious model for the end of time is an intimate death." Richard's end, pitifully confusing the two models, arrives as the intimate aftermath of a secular apocalypse, a Day of Reckoning in Chancery. The ironies of adjudication in *Bleak House* have been active since the false dawn of the opening pages, with its immanent apocalypse, yet sixty-four chapters later Richard's last chapter opens with the sudden hope for a legal judgment day on his living calendar. Even Esther "had sufficient hopes of the Will to be all in a flutter about it," but the only will that is done is the One which ushers to that Kingdom to come of eternal Judgment. Just this side of an infinity that dwindles all space and time, Richard confuses the two in his mind. "When shall I go from this place," he asks, "to that pleasant country where the old times are?" For Richard, since there is no place left to go this side of the grave, the effort at "beginning the world" can only be a retrospective recapturing of the world he has squandered and lost, a now remote world where space and time collapse, just before their vanishing point at infinity, into a dream of restitution and renewal in an unmapped region of the memory. Richard has said "that there is nothing on earth I should so much like to see as their house—Dame Durden's and Woodcourt's house," and his wish vicariously to see another happier marriage localized and housed, this yearning, even by proxy, for temporal closure in marriage, is referred ironically forward to the ultimate closure of his story in death by the figure of speech "nothing on earth." Death is a verbal disinterring in Dickens, as we have repeatedly seen, and it can resuscitate, however despairingly, the dustiest phrases. Even a verb like "marry" is poignantly reinvested in this lethal context. "I have married you to poverty and trouble," he says to Ada, using this sacred term as a metaphor for bondage, a wedding not to a man but to those fitful, self-defeating aspirations into which his very self has vanished; such a marriage is a dead end, not a serene closing off of the will, and just before his human end he thirsts for the vision of something better. Just as with the relationship between Pip and Little Pip in *Great Expectations*—a point central to Said's reading of the novel as a study in psychic beginnings—authentic selfhood for such characters can only be initiated and launched at one remove, through a beginning devolved upon the second generation that is also, for the originating self, an end: emotional stasis for Pip, with death around the corner from fictional closure, and actual death onstage for Richard.

In his clinging emphasis on starting afresh, Richard hopes to "prepare myself to be a guide to my unborn child," and since we anticipate the terminal initiative he is about to take, the phrase resonates against his doom; he will not only, in death, be a perpetual object lesson to his child, an example of the perverse vitiation of youthful desire, but more immediately he may even, from his imminent position outside of life, be able to usher his son to the borders of the living world. Not only are the ideas of initiation, marriage, and guidance to the unborn redefined by the muted despair of this death scene, but as with "Jo's Will" before it, and more recently in Lady Dedlock's death message, the "hopes of the Will" that began the chapter only to be exploded in Chancery have returned for Richard's bequest of double apology to Jarndyce and to Ada, the only thing he too has to leave behind him. Lady Dedlock's last words, in a note given to Guster for delivery to Esther, were "Farewell. Forgive." Grammatically and spiritually, the second is the imperative of her salvation, and yet it seems alert to more than a simple "Forgive me." Its underspecification argues breadth. As in the case of Jo, who asked for Esther's forgiveness and immediately gave up the world in the midst of a prayer that understands absolution as at one with the forgiving of those who trespass against us, so Lady Dedlock seems to partake of this universal invocation of mercy. Let us all forgive each other for the love we evacuate from our lives. Richard's death also resembles those of Jo and Lady Dedlock, and other dyings as well, in the imagery that accompanies this motif of contrition. Jo's last words are spoken in a darkness awaiting light, and after Lady Dedlock's final note, written "almost in the dark," she too may get a glimpse of a glimmer on the other shore—for she is found dead as "the morning faintly struggled in." As with Jo, her "dark benighted way" is, if only dimly, alleviated by light at its end. We remember of course, on the other hand, the risen shadow at Gridley's death, the guttering down and out of the candle at Nemo's, and at Tulkinghorn's those "two candles that were blown out suddenly, soon after being lit"—extinguished, we assume, either deliberately by his murderer or by the force of the gunshot. Put out the light and then, instantaneously, put out the light.

Richard, like Jo and even Lady Dedlock, since he too has time to purge his soul in apology, deserves a poetic justice at least somewhat less austere, a rigor warmed by ambiguity. The "light in his eyes" when Richard first exclaims "I will begin the world" (himself ambiguously the object or the subjective source of the radiance, as in the difference between light beamed *into* and gleaming *from*) has not by the time of his last speech blotted out, or blinded him to, the emotional darkness he has wrought—and wreaked upon his wife: "I have fallen like a poor stray shadow on your way. . . . You will forgive me all this, my Ada, before I begin the world?" The irony of "beginning" speeds its way to eternity in the next paragraph: "A smile irradiated his face, as she bent to kiss him. He slowly laid his face down upon her bosom, drew his arms closer round her neck, and with one parting sob began the world. Not this world, O not this! The world that sets this right!" That uncertainly external or inward gleam, the glimmer of ambiguous hope in the earlier phrase "light in his eyes," has now become an "irradiating" brilliance unquestionably reflected in his eyes from within, a simple metaphor for a smile. And yet Richard's dying delusion about beginning "this world" is confidently corrected, after an interval of negation ("not this world") by an unhesitant vision of an otherworld. It is one of the most economically explicit witnesses to a Christian afterlife in Dickens, certainly the only unequivocal claim for one registered in *Bleak House,* with the idiom for coming into majority urged over into an infinite futurity. Of course the narrative voice is, for the first time in the onstage death scenes since that of Gridley, Esther's voice, not Dickens's and it is in her generous imagination that the "shadow" the earlier death seemed to cast on Richard's and Ada's life has now been eradicated by a brightness from, at once, within and beyond. Esther is of course a narrator with an earnest stake in beginnings— namely that of her own arrived identity in the world—and it is the voice of her flourishing new confidence in what can be begun anew, not Dickens's guarded phrasing, which guides Richard to his Judgment.

But the chapter has one more paragraph, one more deliberately uneditorialized statement, uncertainly hung from the rubric "Beginning the World" and uncompromisingly problematic with regard to the question of exits and ends: "When all was still, at a late hour, poor crazed Miss Flite came weeping to me, and told me she had given her birds their liberty." It has been the lifelong vow of this prophetess of the legal bureaucracy that release will come only with judgment. It is a judgment apocalyptically imagined, couched from the start in Biblical terms. " 'I positively doubt,' says Miss Flite, 'I do assure you, whether while matters are still unsettled, and the sixth or Great Seal still prevails, *I* may not one day be found lying stark and senseless here, as I have found so many birds!' " Of course life must always be contingent, "unsettled," and the monomaniacal wait for the seventh seal of Revelation is only her preparation for a private doomsday. Is this what we get in the last paragraph of "Beginning the World"? Clearly this flighty woman, her wits long flown, hypothetically identifies her eventual fate with that of her birds. Is this identification implied in their release as well? Is it a genuine coming into her name by taking flight? And what, if so, does that mean? Escape, or death, or the one as metaphor for the other? Dickens would have been more than capable of deftly inserting a line or two in the concluding chapter about Miss Flite's freedom from monomania into serene old age, a benign dotage, her dark ubiquity exchanged for a kind of grandmotherly presence at the Bleak House hearth; Welsh might rightly have read such completion, such stasis, as moving toward and amounting to death. Dickens would also have been capable of dispatching Miss Flite to eternity in a line or a paragraph, her festered attachment to the court, like Gridley's before her, too poisonously ingrained for anything but fatal severance. Is her uncaging an apocalyptic and tacitly suicidal gesture, then, or a reawakening to the mundane world and its healthier possibilities, its unfevered freedoms? Since we hear not a word more about her, the questions ordinarily raised by an attempt to psychologize closure or take theoretical stock of it become, given how precipitously the narrative drops away from her, acute and crucial in the case of Miss Flite.

In Ruskin's checklist of exits from *Bleak House,* he recalls that Miss Flite either dies of "insanity" or is one of those characters "left for death's, in the drop scene." Yet is it madness that releases the birds, or its end? And does the self, so long a function of that madness, have nothing left to call its own when the energy of obsession, as it was for Gridley, is swept suddenly away? This may well be the inexorable logic of Dickens's truncated plot line at this point. Perhaps Ruskin has stumbled on a truth which narrative silence articulates, unspoken closure confirms; if so, the truth would be deeply compatible with that morality of death which Ruskin is so consistently oblivious to in Dickens's intrepid symbolism. As with Gridley who died without her blessing, once Miss Flite's *idée fixe* is extirpated after so much mortification and waste, her emancipation of the birds may well be taken reflexively to stand for her own absolute release, a Judgment no longer shrunken to judicial lower case—the narrative itself struck into silence for a death scene by implication in a novel full of corpses.

Richard Carstone wants, like nothing on earth, to contemplate marriage and domestic retreat. According to Alexander Welsh, we might say that in traditional novels characters die to get married; here Richard dies for them. Instead of starting over, with Esther and Allan as prototypes, Richard is initiated into the otherworld. With one novelistic option for end-stopping on his mind, his death actually exemplifies the alternative mode. And immediately upon this implied investigation of death and marriage as interchangeable closures, there is that premature silence about Miss Flite. Death can be seen simply as an end to life as it has been lived, the release from a *raison d'être,* with the curtain brought down not on a character so much as on a process of characterization. Forster's most interesting remark about such matters happens to come not in *Aspects of the Novel* but in a comment by Adela Quested in *A Passage to India:* "I used to feel death selected people, it is a notion one gets from novels, because some of the characters are usually left talking at the end." Or left mutely in the wings. And so we are back again with Miss Flite and the implications of silence, by and about characters. It is the silence from which they emerge in the first place. In the proliferated death scenes of *Bleak House,* Dickens brings death as never before into the pages that intervene between the implied oblivion before and after the arc of story, the unvoiced voids of narrative.

In this rich middle ground death furrows and fertilizes Dickensian psychology. His agnostic candor, embroiled always with a nostalgia for immortality, gives his death scenes a spiritual leanness and symbolic economy that also pitch ambivalently beyond, while never forgetting that the only judgment a novelist can afford to care about aesthetically is the one rendered by death, not after it. In the ordering and portent of his death scenes Dickens tapped as no writer of fiction before him the profound, sometimes meliorating, more often astringent relation between the antonyms latent in the noun "mortality," a functional pun denoting both the condition of human life and, in a definition only recently obsolete for Dickens, its end in death. This linguistic curiosity suggests at once a pervasive narrative strategy, a fictional psychology, and an entire satiric method. Life, that is, fluctuates with or is intercut with death in the ordinary mimetic thread of plot; death informs the mentality of the living; death can also be, in a pathetic or condemnatory sense, synonymous with life, existence itself the slow succumbing to a mortal wound usually self-induced.

We are told that death can relive life while relieving it of the burden of consciousness. Rumor has it, for example, that for a drowning man death is a rehearsal of an entire life. Dickens's interest, more often than not, lies oppositely with the ironic special case of lives so empty that they are merely extended rehearsals for death. Seen from within, death may replay life; seen from without, death can display the nature of that life to the audience of satire or tragedy, becoming a protracted simile for life gone defunct. When the effects of death as a narrative event and as a metaphor converge in Dickens, death can truncate one strand of a plot with, in both senses, a summary judgment, whereby the manner of death and the deadliness itself visualize and evaluate the quality of life. Death by epitome, especially of this narrative sort, is Dickens's great symbolic contribution to the New Mortality of the nineteenth-century novel.

If it is not too late to say "in short" with a straight face, *The Ancient Mariner*'s spectral personification of "LIFE-IN-DEATH" presides over the demises of *Bleak House* like a tutelary demon, while the thanatology of the novel is, one might also say, coterminous with the psychology of its heroine. In no other novel by Dickens, quite possibly in no other work in English of the nineteenth century, is the moribund so severely, so severally, exposed as a *modus vivendi*. And as never so completely before, Dickens's corpses, spiritual until they become literal, are deployed around a heroine's central "struggle into being." The phrase is Lawrence's for the characters of Hardy, and these are indeed two authors most directly in this Dickensian tradition of symbolic death scenes, along with Conrad, Forster, Woolf, and Beckett. As much as any other form of fictional innovation, the metaphoric death warrant is the stamp of Dickens's modernism, and the anxieties of his heroine, Esther Summerson, involve her in a distinctly modernist struggle to keep the proximity of death from becoming death by proxy. Walter Benjamin has written eloquently that we go to the novel "not because it presents someone else's fate to us, perhaps didactically, but because this stranger's fate by virtue of the flame which consumes it yields us the warmth which we never draw from our own fate. What draws the reader to the novel is the hope of warming his shivering life with a death he reads about." Yet within the novels of Dickens and his successors, what often draws a character, consciously or not, to the death of another, or arranges deaths around a problematic life, derives from a colder logic. Inside fiction, tentative or inauthentic vitality can be chilled to panic, even to recognition, by a death it confronts. This is merely one of the ways Dickens's novels demonstrate that death in fiction punctuates life not only by providing its full stop, but by exclaiming upon it and interrogating it. Hence death's aesthetic utility, its cruel beauty.

Endings

John Kucich

The most obvious question left unsettled by the ending of *Bleak House* is, how do we evaluate Esther's marriage, especially as it is conceived symbolically, through her transition to a second Bleak House? The question seems crucial in light of the ground-clearing tone to the end of the novel. Lady Dedlock and Richard Carstone, chief victims of the law, are dead; Tulkinghorn, its emanation, is dead; the Jarndyce suit is dead; all dangerous secrets are laid to rest. What, then, after this partial catharsis of the Chancery plot, is the concluding action in Esther's plot—is it a rebirth, a reenactment, or an evasion?

The more disturbing possibility is that this marriage is simply the way things happen to Esther, that is, that her marriage means something to her, and something else in our terms or in the terms of the third-person narrator. The question of the reliability of Esther's happiness in the ending reflects problems in our ability to evaluate her role in the novel all the way through. After all, not only do we know little about Esther's second house, but our judgment of her first is also clouded by ambiguities. Throughout the novel, there are ominous parallels between her world and the world of the third-person narrator. What is the difference, for example, between the chaos of Chancery and the "pleasant irregularity" of Esther's Bleak House? Certainly, too, Esther's mind is a labyrinth; it is difficult to estimate the emotional cost of her compulsive deference and self-denial. More seriously, as we saw [elsewhere], how much of that

From *Excess and Restraint in the Novels of Charles Dickens.* © 1981 by the University of Georgia Press.

self-denial conceals a will to power? Esther's egotism has bothered many readers, but still more disturbing is the way Esther's control of others echoes Tulkinghorn's. Both are in everyone's confidence yet tell nothing about their own deeper intentions; both have a collection of keys and locks; both harp on their all-justifying sense of duty; both hold onto the fates of others by holding onto their letters—Tulkinghorn blackmails with Captain Hawdon's letters, and Esther keeps Jarndyce's letter proposing marriage for a month before she answers it. Of course, there is never any doubt whose side Dickens is on. Nevertheless, these strange, insistent resonances, by making Esther herself ambiguous, make it difficult to specify what kind of change—or what kind of repetition—is involved in the most prominent action of the ending, Esther's movement from one Bleak House to another.

Evidently, *Bleak House* would make Richard Carstones of us all. Rather than muddling through all these ambiguities, though, we can retreat to the most abstract level to make Esther's matrimonial pattern a little clearer. The most significant repetition of all is a repetition of sexual triangles that frames the entire novel. The triad of Sir Leicester, Lady Dedlock, and Captain Hawdon that is ultimately at the source of almost everything in the book—it even marks Esther's conception—is reworked in the sexual triangle at the end of the second plot, that of Jarndyce, Esther, and Woodcourt. The configurations are not readily apparent, but they mesh in interesting ways. For one thing, both triangles involve transitions between an older man and a younger one—Dickens's generational theme—and both involve transitions between a husband, or near-husband, and a lover—problems of adultery; for another, in both cases the forbidden lover is the more attractive: Lady Dedlock's affair with Captain Hawdon takes place against a background of social exhaustion and a dull marriage to a man old enough to be her father, while Esther's attraction to *her* sailor is placed against her betrothal to an aging father-figure, a cloying betrothal that "made no difference." As denials of passionate love, though, we should note that both the Dedlock marriage and Esther's betrothal to Jarndyce also contain a kind of tender affection that positively stresses the value of conservative, as opposed to excessive, love. Sir Leicester, surprisingly, forgives Lady Dedlock in a gesture that actually foreshadows Jarndyce's own self-sacrifice.

What makes this repetition of triangles important is the obvious difference: the three characters of the first triangle are destroyed by social and moral constraints, while the second triangle works. It does not work as a *ménage à trois,* exactly, but it does feature a woman's sexual transition from one man to another, without doing violence to the first, more paternal relationship. The second triangle features a breakthrough, an expending of Esther's sexual energies beyond their confinement to Jarndyce, the same kind of surpassing of sexual boundaries that, in its original form, was the novel's great transgression. The inhibition and paralysis in the first triangle—defenses against transgression that are repeated in Esther's own obsessive self-denial, which is an indirect response to Lady Dedlock's excesses that keeps her from Woodcourt—are broken, however abstractly, by the successful, excessive action in the second triangle.

The kind of freedom Esther achieves is nonspecific and expansive, which makes it congruent with our previous notion of release, as a close look at the kind of action she and Lady Dedlock share will demonstrate. Lady Dedlock's sin, of course, is sexual, and the sexual act itself is an experience of an intense destruction of boundaries, a literal penetration of the limits of bodily identity. On another level, though, as we have seen, both Lady Dedlock's sin and Esther's marriage confuse problems of adultery and generational transition. There appears to be a failure on Dickens's part to be explicit, to spell out the nature of the sexual conflict—a vagueness which often makes Dickens subject to analyses like Françoise Basch's description of the Victorians' "systematic confusion of sexual roles" as a defense against female sexuality. But in this instance Dickens's vagueness has a deeper purpose. Sex is not *the* issue in this novel. It is subsumed in a more general context of restlessness, constraint, limitation, and needs for release from boundaries.

To make the broader range of problems of boundaries clear, we need only cull other echoes from the novel, which are plentiful. Caddy Jellyby, for example, also struggles with the narrowly generational problem. Frustrated at home by parents who enslave her and who are incapable of receiving her love, Caddy escapes to a husband. That Prince Turveydrop brings in tow a father to whose nourishment Caddy dedicates herself is for her a compromise between excess and moral restraint, a mixture of sexual gratification and duty. George the Trooper is a more interesting case, though, in that George presents a problem of excessive, rebellious energy that is specifically nonsexual. Like so many other children in this novel—

Caddy, Richard, the Pardiggle brood—George is unable to reconcile the restraints of his family circle with his restless drives. But George's desires have no sexual object; in fact, they have no object at all. Like Richard, George is pure restlessness. Feeling "smothered" is his favorite response to his problems. His presence in the novel suggests a primary need to vent rebellious energy; specifically, George has no particular dissatisfaction with the Rouncewell family; he simply *has to go*.

Seen in the light of primary restlessness, the polar opposition of social institutions and the individual—such a constant theme of Dickens criticism—breaks down. In *Bleak House,* both the individual and society are motivated by similar energies; the Jarndyce suit, for instance, is reckless growth, a blind, expansive force, an appetite that breaks down and consumes all obstacles to itself. Bucket, too, the arm of the institution, presents a similar problem of restless and unconstrained—because sanctioned— energy. Critics who tend to oppose social systems to the individual in Dickens also tend to see Bucket only as a force for social order, neglecting to see that Bucket thrives on conflict and on overcoming others, not on regularity.

In a novel so saturated with the crushing weight of blackmail, repression, imprisonment, and legal dungeons, it is not easy to see— except in characters like Bucket, George, Richard, or Gridley—that there is also present a certain primary kind of energy randomly seeking to break limits. Of course, it would be nonsense to claim that the problem for Esther and for Lady Dedlock is simply what to do with their excess energy, as if there were not a spectrum of motives involved. Still, both are driven by energies whose source it is difficult to locate as a response to anything: Lady Dedlock's social ambition, and Esther's obsession with her own saintliness. These drives have a life of their own which is bent into even more concrete motivations as they encounter particular kinds of restraints. Lady Dedlock's frigidity is her weapon against the Fashionable Intelligence; Esther's self-denial is the method she learns from her Calvinist upbringing and uses against its ethos of self-obliteration. Lady Dedlock's and Esther's more important and more distinctly personal motives, though, arise only when they confront the fact that drives for unqualified release—as figured in characters like Bucket or Skimpole, or in themselves—threaten both their lives and those of their loved ones. The problem for Esther, for Lady Dedlock, for George, and for all the good characters, is how to reconcile desires for expenditure with their resistance to the cruelty and the violence of expenditure. They all must somehow reconcile drives toward release with a conservative structure of affection and love.

Lady Dedlock, of course, fails; so does Richard. But a character like George does gratify both his impulse to exceed his family circle and his love for his family by the end of the novel in a way that was not available to him in the beginning. Instead of running away and sinking his energy into useless service in the army, George again leaves his family—after getting their approval this time—and promptly binds himself to Sir Leicester. This particular release and immediate binding of energy makes more emotional sense to us than a career in the army does, now that we have seen Sir Leicester's tender side. Significantly, too, George insists on geographical separation from his family, yet he remains near them. Seen in this light, George's compromise provides us with the key to the mystery of the two Bleak Houses and the reason why Jarndyce's relationship to Esther and Woodcourt must be preserved: Esther and Woodcourt, too, remain geographically separate, yet near Jarndyce, in a house that repeats his. The second Bleak House represents a movement out of stability—an explicitly sexual movement—yet it retains its tie to the first. It is imbalance-within-balance; excess is brought in under cover of stability.

Before we consider whether Esther's marriage is a workable strategy that resolves problems of release and restraint, however, it is important to see first how the narrative logic puts the reader on the side of the expenditure, rather than against it. We never question the logic of Esther's transition to Woodcourt; we may doubt that the final arrangement is as completely happy as Esther would have us believe, but there is no question that Esther's transition is something to be approved as natural—emotionally or in narrative terms. For this purpose, the narrative context carefully sets up conditions for plausibility. First, the overwhelming atmosphere of mutual deference in *Bleak House* makes the resolution seem appropriate for the characters, rather than either a merely fanciful, merely fairy-tale resolution, or an excessively violent change. None of the characters involved contorts himself in any way—at least, given what we know of them. On the contrary, they all seem to produce the resolution inevitably. In a strange way, Jarndyce's own system of self-denial, which Esther has adulated and deferred to throughout the novel in precedent-setting ways, fittingly prevails again over hers and seems to lead him logically to anticipate her needs. At the same time, Jarndyce's own relationship to Esther is desexualized well enough to minimize conflict between himself and Woodcourt. Second, the reader is made to expect such a resolution because of the glaring "mistake" threatened by Esther's quasi-incestuous betrothal to Jarndyce. We are made to hope that Jarndyce will turn her over to Woodcourt and, when he does, it seems both to relieve us and to confirm our expectations rather than to play havoc with our sense of reality. Third, Jarndyce himself is not abandoned; rather, he is restored to his original, benign position by the introduction of Ada in her new relationship to him as her "guardian." Finally, the only voice of social opposition, Mrs. Woodcourt's, is made both harmless enough and unpleasant enough for us to wish for her to be overcome. In short, because of the narrative logic and also because there is a displacement in our awareness of conflict away from the sexual problem toward the conflict in Esther's own internal integration of desire and passivity—a conflict that does not play any obvious role in Jarndyce's decision—it is easier to believe that Esther's transition to Woodcourt is right for all three characters than to decide just what it is about any of it that bothers us. This transition, which dissolves Esther's confinement to Jarndyce, is possibly the greatest successful action in *Bleak House,* and the reader experiences it as an unqualified, good release.

Beyond the purely circumstantial framework for Esther's transition, the marriage is also presented as an appropriate resolution because, like George's service of Sir Leicester or Caddy's marriage, it is fused with symbolic terms for restraint. For one thing, Esther's transition is acceptable because, despite her desire for it, she is capable of renouncing it. Release operates through her, rather than involving her in the guilt of self-willed freedom. More importantly, because we have been made to feel that Esther's devotion to duty and her militantly organized self-denial is too good and actually does her harm, it is refreshing to think that she can afford to lose some of that control. As for Jarndyce, his self-denial, which borders on being a new problem of limitation, is transfigured as an expenditure; he gives Esther to Woodcourt, and this act of deliberate loss affords him the kind of satisfaction he has been able to take through pure generosity all along. In this transition, then, the poles of limitation and release are combined symbolically in a way that resolves the initial problem.

At the same time, this "harmony" remains one of symbolic adjustment; it does not leave us with a prescription. Esther's marriage is felt as a success through the symbolic drama, but as an action it cannot be reduced to a formula for action. The addition of a Growlery for Jarndyce (and it is significant that it is a Growlery Jarndyce is consigned to) in the second house is not a worldly strategy; Sir Leicester, for example, would probably not have felt comfortable living with Lady Dedlock and Captain Hawdon in Krook's rag-and-bottle shop, even if they gave him his own room. The absurdity bears heavily on the possibility that Esther's marriage "solves" conflict; by shifting the two situations slightly, the novel never invites a direct comparison. The conditions of Esther's triangle are rearranged so that impediments can be reasonably overcome, and we accept the expansive movement of the second triangle without seeing it specifically as a redemption of the first. It is an act that makes logical sense, that resolves a symbolic dilemma, that provides a localized release from restrictions; it is not a solution.

Though elaborately idiosyncratic, Esther's successful sexual transition in *Bleak House* is not an isolated instance of this kind of resolution. Whenever Dickens uses sexual triangles, he always manages to permit a triumphant spilling over of erotic energies that remains enigmatically singular. In *David Copperfield*, we are explicitly warned against the transferability of love through Little Em'ly, who throws over Ham for Steerforth, and through Annie, who is almost lured away from Dr. Strong by the seducer Jack Maldon. Then, too, Mrs. Copperfield's second marriage becomes, in effect, a betrayal of David, and Betsey Trotwood is forced to remain single—in a celibate relationship to Mr. Dick—as if in punishment for her bad marriage. Romantic restlessness is also satirized through Micawber's comic insistences about his faithfulness to Mrs. Micawber. But through the narrative convenience of Dora's death, David becomes the single character who is able to correct the errors of his first choice and to find a new partner. Marrying Agnes is even made to seem a duty when David learns that their union was Dora's last wish. Though skewed slightly from problems presented by Em'ly, Annie, and the others, David's second marriage satisfies in an elliptic way desires for a liberation of romantic love that the entire novel seems to warn us against. Less strikingly, perhaps, in *Our Mutual Friend,* Eugene

Wrayburn's ability to reject the girl forced on him by his father and to marry Lizzie instead is neutrally counterpointed by Bradley Headstone's disastrous attempt to forego Miss Peecher, who is eventually forced on him by Riderhood as well as by the conventions of class, for Lizzie. And, in the same novel, the balance between excessive or new love and conservative, older love is delicately maintained in a purely symbolic way by the novel's two love plots; while Eugene manages to escape a choice dictated by his father and finds a new mate, John Harmon does the reverse; he succeeds in first transforming and then marrying precisely the girl dictated by parental choice. These two love plots play off the rival satisfactions of excess and restraint in a fictional, nonusable resolution. Still another eccentric solution to the problem of sexual transition concludes *Little Dorrit.* The initial crime, the adultery of Arthur's father, is completed and legitimized in a symbolic way; like his father, Arthur defies his mother's repressive Calvinism by marrying the girl who—solely in terms of his father's will—*stands for* his sinning mother as the next surviving heir. Arthur's love for Little Dorrit thus resurrects the history of his father's adultery and seems to consummate it in a morally satisfying way while it shifts the burden of guilt in the novel to the repressive Mrs. Clennam. Thus, the rebellious liberation of his father's erotic energy is fulfilled by Arthur's innocent love for Little Dorrit and by the corresponding guilt of Mrs. Clennam, who represents moral authority and restraint.

As these novels demonstrate, release and restraint are, in their ultimate extension, adjacent values; there is no way to test the ethical status of Dickens's successful triangles as integrated acts that can be repeated. These triangles remain a kind of stored potential, a delicate attitudinal disposition, an image, an inclination. It is impossible to say whether the same kind of resolution is translatable outward. In *Bleak House,* for example, the success of Esther's triangle does seem to be repeated in George's retainership, and in the Turveydrops, and in Matthew Bagnet's channeling of his martial spirit into "blasting away" at his bassoon; but these secondary resolutions, imitating the main one, border on being grotesque parodies. George's invisible iron spurs, for instance, ominously echo Mr. Rouncewell's iron mills (that one of these brothers should have only a first name, and the other only a last name, is an emblem of permanent dislocation); the factory, which combines progress and unrestrained energy with social use, is Dickens's most disturbing image in this novel of safely reconciled expenditure and conservation. It goes without saying, too, that George's role as retainer is mildly pathetic. In a more direct failure, the Turveydrops' marriage results in a stunted, deaf-mute child. Boythorn, too, is forever divided against himself and against Sir Leicester in a burlesque of violent energy linked to good intentions; he cannot escape his split persona, even though he wants to. The inescapable fact for Dickens in *Bleak House*—as in all his novels—is that any synthesis of violence and order will be a contortion, a kind of internal combustion. The form left over by compromise always seems warped and can be as potentially dangerous as active transgression. Symbolic resolutions, too—like the texture of Esther's narrative, which reorganizes verbally the discordant world of the third-person narrator—are always very delicate and idiosyncratic.

Through such pressing insistence on instability and impossible opposition, the Dickens ending never really ends; *Bleak House* does not reconcile conflicts in any absolute way, not even in Esther's marriage. The instability of any permanent resolution is summed up in the last hanging, unresolved sentence. Do we take Woodcourt's flattery as a well-meaning matrimonial lie, but a lie nevertheless, one that conceals his disappointment with Esther's looks and, potentially, his failure to satisfy and contain his desires in her? Or do we take it as a complete release from any mortal interest in human beauty? As for Esther in this last scene, what of her final flirtation with egotism? The complex of mirror images in the book has suggested all along that Esther's continual destruction of her own selfish limitations is actually, in part, an economy of petty self-righteousness and self-aggrandizement.

Instability, madness even, is at the heart of this novel. But that Esther's life conceals—imperfectly—a radical instability is not to say that she is its victim. Through Esther, the novel builds a kind of attitudinal potency by developing a sexual transition that was hopelessly blocked in the beginning. Whatever the consequences, Esther has broken through the barrier of that sexual conflict in a very real way. Rather than merely repeating Lady Dedlock's muddle, she has broken with it and has made her life what her first chapter called it, "A Progress."

The Occult in *Bleak House*

Christopher Herbert

The condition of England . . . is justly regarded as one of the most ominous, and withal one of the strangest, ever seen in this world.

CARLYLE, Past and Present

"In Bleak House," Dickens declares in a provocative and now much-discussed formula, though one that still needs elucidation, "I have purposely dwelt upon the romantic side of familiar things." First there is the stress on "purposely": the radically mixed technique of this novel, Dickens is insisting, is a deliberate, conscious invention with its own artistic purpose—though what this is he leaves for the moment unexplained. He is seeking with this adverb to protect himself against the perennial assumption, lately revived, that what Henry James called the "fantastic" vein in his fiction is simply an uncontrollable reflex akin to hallucination rather than art. But the core of the phrase is his acknowledgment of the peculiarly equivocal quality of *Bleak House,* its constant fusion—or is it fission?—of the "romantic" and the "familiar." Both terms have obvious loci in the text even though their interconnections may at first be enigmatic. On the one hand, as a number of scholars have insisted, *Bleak House* presents itself as a "predominantly topical" work anchored at a hundred places in the familiar, in contemporary actualities; but this topical novel is marked at the same time by a vein of hyperbolic fantasy that veers so sharply away from normal realism as often (in the episode of Spontaneous Combustion, for example) to induce in the reader a kind of esthetic vertigo. Given this powerful tendency to split, so to speak,

From *Novel: A Forum on Fiction* 17, no. 2 (Winter 1984). © 1984 by Novel Corporation.

at the seams, *Bleak House* needs among other things to be seen as a great device designed "purposely" to test the tensile strength of fictional structures.

The configurations of the romantic and the familiar in *Bleak House* are often intricate, but these two poles of Dickens's fictive world are plainly defined from the first in the central device of doubled narrators. The third-person narrator represents among other things the pole of "romantic" vision. From his perspective reality everywhere becomes impregnated with the fantastic and seems, indeed, perpetually on the verge of dissolving into phantasmagoria: forty-foot-long dinosaurs are seen waddling up Holborn Hill, a law court becomes a Pandemonium where lawyers sit in foggy cloudbanks, ghoulish trolls appallingly explode in puffs of slimy smoke. The world reported upon by Esther is different in kind, a world mainly of commonplace fact, a "precise, exact, and orderly" world where all is banal, tangible, "familiar," a world of domestic interiors, household routine, intimate personal relationships. Esther's characteristic domestic chores—keeping the keys, taking inventories of "each little storeroom drawer and cupboard," presiding over "jams, and pickles, and preserves, and bottles"—themselves symbolize in their imagery of containment and systematic regularity her narrative function as the sponsor of a world insulated from the disruptive processes of fantasy that her anonymous co-narrator freely gives rein to. But the center of the novel's dramatic pattern is Esther's step-by-step initiation into seemingly fantastic realities—public realities like Chancery, private ones like the mysteries of hidden identities—and one result is a progressive contamination of her humdrum narrative style by the "romantic." Dickens makes this process into an extended parable of the limitations of what in 1851 had just begun vaingloriously to call itself "realism." Esther's development as a narrator reaches its apogee in the episode of her final walk to the graveyard, where the outward scene—not for the first time in her experience—dissolves entirely in phantasmagoria:

> I recollect the wet house-tops, the clogged and bursting gutters and waterspouts, the mounds of blackened ice and snow. . . . At the same time I remember . . . that the stained house fronts put on human shapes and looked at me; that great water-gates seemed to be opening and clos-

ing in my head, or in the air; and that the unreal things
were more substantial than the real.

This passage calls for detailed commentary, but let us focus here
on its very suggestive last phrase, which distils the essence of Esther's
experience and forms, I think, a very serviceable gloss on Dickens's
own prefatory phrase about "the romantic side of familiar things."
What Esther has discovered about her world is in effect its occultness,
its infestation by "unreal things" that turn out fantastically to be the
realest, most substantial things of all. In what follows I want to plot
as exactly as possible some of the wide-ranging manifestations of this
principle in *Bleak House*. On the most immediate level this means
showing how heavily Dickens relies upon one audacious stylistic
device, the weaving of gothic supernaturalism into this concerted
study of the perturbations of nineteenth-century society. Isolating
this device should help, first, to explain the persistent impression that
readers get of an ominous power of fate or, in one recent critic's
words, of "a sinister, supernatural agency" [Harvey Peter Sucksmith]
hovering over the novel's fictive world, but it should also help us to
see in turn that the supernatural agency of *Bleak House* is just a
many-branched metaphor for his central subject in fiction, the radical
newness and strangeness of nineteenth-century life.

I

Just how deeply the archetypal gothic figure of ghostly haunting
is embedded in *Bleak House* can be seen, again, in the way it suggests
itself in the novel's compound narrative: for in contrast to Esther's
narrative, firmly localized as it is in a narrator of definite identity, a
tangible presence, how can the omniscient narrator strike us if not as
a kind of ghost, an occult disembodied voice haunting the story,
hovering mysteriously overhead at some indeterminate vantage
point, pervading every narrative nook and cranny? Dickens loses no
opportunity to highlight the strangeness of this voice that speaks out
of thin air and magically translates itself from scene to scene "as the
crow flies" in the twinkling of an eye. Almost more than any other
single function, the double narration in *Bleak House* serves to bring to
the surface the inherently fantastic property of omniscient narration—fantastic especially in the context of an occluded world like this
one, where omniscience is scarcely conceivable. In making us newly
conscious of the strangeness of this convention Dickens thus in effect

makes us discover the "romantic side" of this most familiar of storytelling devices; indeed he hints inescapably at the uncanny quality of fiction itself.

But such an effect as this one seems almost serendipitous as a novel that often brings occult mystery into the story in overt, even sensationalistic, forms, as though to advertise the humble literary genealogy of what will become its own richest metaphors. Thus Dickens introduces Chesney Wold as the classic haunted castle of Radcliffean horror romance, a gloomy pile pervaded by "ghosts and mystery" where jittery maidservants have sudden fits of panic and a sharp ear can actually hear the sinister footsteps of the Dedlock family specter prowling the flagstone terrace, the "Ghost Walk." This strain of black magic breaks out again, for example, during the panicky night that Guppy and Jobling spend in the room where Nemo died, feeling themselves to be "haunted by the ghosts of sound— strange cracks and tickings," and seeming to hear about them "the tread of dreadful feet" and "the rustling of garments that have no substance in them." When Mr. Snagsby the law-stationer finds himself drawn into Mr. Tulkinghorn's investigations he is gradually enveloped in the same climate of dread, feeling himself to be haunted by phantasmal pursuers and "wrapped round with secrecy and mystery," as he puts it, "till my life is a burden to me." Jo the crossing sweeper suffers from a superstitious terror of his nemesis Inspector Bucket, who seems to him uncannily to be, like a supernatural being, "in all manner of places, all at wunst," and of the eerie women in black who keep materializing fantastically in his path. These persistent suggestions of occult horror come to a crescendo in the (comic) macabre episode of Mr. Krook's Spontaneous Combustion, an eruption of horrific black magic that might have come from a gothic fantasy like *Melmoth the Wanderer* and that forms by far the most extreme instance of the *Bleak House* project of testing the cohesiveness of the romantic and the familiar. *Bleak House,* in other words, constantly identifies itself as nothing more elevated than a species of ghost story, a thriller in which the occult is always close at hand.

But the ghost story is joined at every point to another, seemingly incompatible mode of fiction, a topical realism that insists fiercely on its own veracity and seriousness as it dwells on problems of modern-day society: poverty, disease, disfunctional institutions. The gothic mystery element in *Bleak House* thus presents itself insistently in the form of a question about disparities of literary "levels," and much of the novel has to do with formulating an answer to precisely this question. Part of the answer lies in understanding the profound connection between Dickens's artistic vocation of sponsoring base, trivialized literary materials (especially those, like ghost stories, with close ties to popular storytelling traditions) and his concurrent sponsorship of the most wretched and forlorn inhabitants of his society: at bottom the two projects are inseparable, as *Bleak House* eloquently suggests. But more to the present point is the specific historical and structural link that appears to connect modern urban–industrial conditions and the fantastic gothicism that enjoyed such a great vogue from the 1790s onward. Wordsworth took such a link for granted, analyzing this (to him, repugnant) style of fiction as dictated by the need of the modern public for the most extreme stimulants to rouse it from the state of "almost savage torpor" caused by "the increasing accumulation of men in cities." Ruskin later brought the same intuition to bear on *Bleak House* itself, seeing the compulsively macabre themes of Dickens's novel as a reflection of morbid sensibilities afflicted by "the monotony of life in the central streets of any great modern city." The defining function of gothic romance, Wordsworth and Ruskin imply, is to procure release by whatever means from the material pressures of the "familiar" in the urban world. *Bleak House* in its audacious mixing of modes emerges as the deepest and most elaborate of all essays on this important juncture of recent literary history, giving us a revelation of the semi-submerged metaphors of modernity informing a half-century of gothic fantasy in literature—a revelation and a brilliant rehabilitation of them too.

This twofold project shows itself most clearly in the figurative device that dominates the novel: the fusing of particular social issues with intimations of occult mystery. Modern problems everywhere take on in Dickens's eyes a *ghostly* aspect, as we see especially in connection with Tom-all-Alone's and the Court of Chancery. Each of these scenes of chaotic disorder is conceived as blackly magical, and monstrous phantasms emanate from each: the typhoid fever of Tom's for example, is "an avenging ghost" invisibly spreading itself throughout the entire kingdom and the many agents of Chancery, notably Tulkinghorn, Bucket, and Vholes, as we shall see, are everywhere figured as occult apparitions, phantoms, "shadows." The vast conspiracy of the law spreads as eerily and as lethally as typhus bacteria. Thus the slum and the Court are intimately associated with each other in the novel's design. The basis of the association is clear: these are two places of surpassing horror, as the stories of victims like Gridley and Jo illustrate. But what gives the horror in each case its strong tinge of occult mystery? To answer this question will take us a long way into the argument of *Bleak House.*

The logic of the supernatural aura surrounding Tom-all-Alone's is precisely suggested, I think, by Freud's analysis of the uncanny as the resurgence of "something familiar and old-established in the mind that has become alienated from it only through the process of repression." Social disorders of the kind epitomized by Tom's, the disorders of devastating poverty, take on a ghostly and terrifying aspect, Dickens implies throughout *Bleak House,* just because they are habitually *repressed*—that is, because of their almost fantastic ability, given the system of modern life, to remain unseen even when existing on the most enormous scale and in plain sight. Tom's represents a whole invisible nether world of poverty and despair lying unnoticed in the midst of the mid-century prosperity of which it is a perhaps necessary byproduct. Mr. Snagsby has lived all his life a few minutes' walk from Tom's without ever having the faintest suspicion of its existence, and when he sees it for the first time he has the impression of stepping into a fantastic, appalling underworld. The invisibility of such an immense and significant fact as Tom's is largely a function of what Dickens evokes so powerfully in this and other novels, the all-enveloping secrecy of a modern city. What fairly obsesses him in *Bleak House,* however, is the concerted will among the literate, pious, and well-to-do to ignore the dark side of contemporary life, and especially to ignore the problem that Dickens recognizes as the hallmark of the age, the misery of the poor. In *Bleak House* this practice of self-deception is portrayed as an integral function of modern capitalistic Christian society. The novel represents ordinary English life as weirdly illusionistic, resting upon a huge conspiracy to pretend that the world of the poor does not exist. The ghost metaphor enters this area of the novel as a crux of Dickens's effort to fathom this conspiracy, which he imagines in the guise of a great system of black magic that effectively condemns the poor to a limbo of unreality. On one level the gothic strain here implies the dark cloud of guilt that hidden poverty throws over modern life; on another it suggests that the price of ignoring such terrible realities is to be haunted and frightened by them. The wretched inhabitants of Tom's swirl before Snagsby's eyes like a swarm of phantoms or "like

a dream of horrible faces" and breed a miasma of disease from which
no one is immune. They represent the most pitiable but also the most
sinister and terrifying secret of the Victorian world, and so become
figures of "romantic" horror.

We reach these images of horror through a wealth of ironic
analysis, notably in Dickens's extended satire of Victorian philanthropy, portrayed here as a system functioning primarily to disguise
the true extent and significance of modern poverty. Organized benevolence becomes in this view another of the systems of exploitation and parasitism that prevail in *Bleak House*. Mrs. Jellyby's
"telescopic" philanthropy is an elaborate strategy for ignoring as
though they didn't exist glaring social evils much closer to home
than Africa, and in a similar way Mrs. Pardiggle in effect discounts
the miseries of her clients by seeing them as nothing but evidence of
moral failings (and of her own moral superiority). Parliament like-
wise discharges its responsibility for the welfare of the people by
showing total unconsciousness of the poor "dying . . . around us
every day" in droves. A much more surprising case of the same
obstructed vision is that of Esther Summerson herself, whose devotion to unselfish good works is at first connected to a sunny naïve
optimism that blinds her, also, to harshly visible realities. Dickens
underlines this point in the scene of Esther's first visit to London,
where her delight at the bustling spectacle of the city streets is only
heightened when she remarks cheerfully on a number of "extraordinary creatures in rags, secretly groping among the swept-out rubbish for pins and other refuse." That she has had a plain view of the
hidden world of urban poverty in its most sickening form she seems
blithely unaware. For a moment Esther thus displays from sheer
naïvete the same moral outlook as the most despicable figure in the
tale, Harold Skimpole, who fondly speaks at one point of the pic-
turesqueness of slaves working the fields of American plantations:
"they people the landscape for me, they give it a poetry for me."
That even Esther could momentarily fall prey to such a view gives
point to Dickens's idea of the masses of the poor as ghosts, all around
us and somehow faceless, anonymous, invisible, even when they
stand before us in plain daylight.

The other principal strain of the occult in Dickens's study of
social disorders is tied to his intuition that they originate in no tangible or manageable causes, but rather in the remote workings of
vast, complex, totally impersonal social and institutional systems

that not only baffle comprehension but seem to function with a menacing, all-pervading life of their own. The "romantic side" of *Bleak House* is inseparable, in other words, from what Raymond Williams identifies as the leading theme of Victorian fiction, the confrontation with "an unknown, unknowable, overwhelming society." Thus the sad plight of Tom-all-Alone's is discovered to be linked to the machinations of Chancery, which in Dickens's fable exemplifies the amazing processes of modern mass society by proving to be of almost infinite ramifications, and to be wholly outside the voluntary control of any individual. In this world all-engulfing social systems function according to their own internal principles, to which human will is irrelevant. Thus, for example, the Lord High Chancellor, the presiding official of a cruelly rapacious institution, turns out in his own person to be "both courtly and kind," a paradox designed to dramatize the point that Chancery is in some fashion driven by a malignant purpose of its own far larger than any motives of individuals.

This is just the issue focussed upon by Gridley, the aggrieved Chancery suitor from Shropshire, who heaps scorn on the supposedly absurd notion that some abstract entity called "the system" is to blame for his ruin. "The system!" he rails. "I am told, on all hands, it's the system. I mustn't look to individuals. It's the system." Dickens sympathizes with Gridley's plea for moral accountability; but he leaves no doubt that his belief in simple tangible realities is hopelessly anachronistic in reference to modern institutions: by virtue of their almost incomprehensible scale they are impersonal and mysterious. In Chancery, as Esther says, there is "no reality in the whole scene." On the surface she is signalling another major instance in which unpleasant facts are blocked from consciousness (none of the officials of Chancery seem to have the slightest awareness that their court is "held in universal horror, contempt, and indignation"). Esther's remark also implies a still deeper insight into the fundamentally occult nature of the power of modern "systems" like this one, power that operates with devastating effect but that has no tangible or intelligible form and is wielded by no one in particular. All one can observe directly of the workings of Chancery is a preposterous farce. It is played out in a London courtroom where lawyers haggle over "bills, cross-bills, answers, rejoinders, injunctions, affidavits," and suchlike procedural technicalities; the unseen reality of Chancery, on the other hand, lies in "its decaying houses and its blighted lands in every shire; . . . its worn-out lunatic in every madhouse, and its dead in every churchyard." The bewildering gap between the trivial cause and the far-flung lethal effects is thus the point which Dickens stresses, for it is precisely here that the occult operation of modern institutional systems manifests itself.

This underlying argument comes vividly into focus, then, in Dickens's conceit of the great Chancery lawsuit Jarndyce and Jarndyce as a supernatural mystery, the very embodiment of the fearfulness that this novel finds in ordinary modern life. What gives the lawsuit its potency as a fictional device is Dickens's idea of presenting it, like the typhoid of Tom's, as a kind of fantastic bodiless living creature, a "Monster" with the ghostly ability to pervade the whole world and to cast its evil spell nearly everywhere. "How many people . . . Jarndyce and Jarndyce has stretched forth its unwholesome land to spoil and corrupt," comments the narrator, stressing the metaphor of the lawsuit as an occult monster, "would be a very wide question." John Jarndyce, full of superstitious fear toward Jarndyce and Jarndyce, calls it "the horrible phantom" of his family, and Miss Flite sees it even more frighteningly in just the same terms. For her, the court with all its procedural mysteries is more than a scene of confusion and venality; it is a nightmare of black magic. The Mace and Seal, she announces, are "cold and glittering devils" with the uncanny power to "draw people on. . . . Draw peace out of them. Sense out of them. Good looks out of them. Good qualities out of them." How justified her imagery of magical vampirism is we come to see in the figure of Mr. Vholes the lawyer, the incarnation, in effect, of the operations of Jarndyce and Jarndyce. Outwardly commonplace, he is the agent of an occult system, and thus he keeps ballooning before our eyes into an image of ghostly terror. His "dead glove," says Esther, "scarcely seemed to have any hand in it"; with his "lifeless manner" and his "pinched lips that looked as if they were cold," he is seen in one nightmarish scene as the very image of supernatural terror, Death in person, come with his "gaunt pale horse" to carry Rick Carstone off into the darkness. The gothic romanticizing of familiar things like lawyers and lawsuits could scarcely be carried further than this.

This constant fusion of occult fantasy and modern social realities in *Bleak House* points finally to quite a different theory of gothic romance from the invidious one shared by Wordsworth and Ruskin. Rather than affording pleasurably exciting escape from the supposed "torpor" and "monotony" of contemporary life, Dickens suggests, ghost fiction strikes a chord of reality by exposing a feeling of latent panic unexpectedly running beneath the surface of the nineteenth-century world; the feeling is wholly at odds with the overt mood of England—"this boastful island"—in the glorious, prosperous Great Exhibition year of 1851. The melodramatic "sensation" plot of *Bleak House* centers almost obsessively on the process of bringing deeply buried facts to light, and the plot thus conceived is itself an elaborate metaphor for this deeper function of the novel, the revelation in figurative language of the secret terror of life in puritan England in the aftermath of the industrial revolution.

II

The same gothic-horror motifs that predominate in Dickens's vision of the external, "topical" sphere of *Bleak House* also turn out to predominate in its psychological one—to such an extent indeed that the two spheres tend persistently, in what seems at first like an artistic confusion, to collapse inextricably into one another. That this effect is a deliberate one is suggested by Miss Flite's explanation of Chancery's mysterious power, which lies wholly, she says, in its appeal to its victims' psyches. "[T]here's a dreadful attraction in the place," she warns Esther. "There's a cruel attraction in the place. You *can't* leave it. And you *must* expect." What exactly gives the "monstrous maze"of Chancery, a byword for hopelessness and certain ruin, its occult and irresistible fascination for suitors like Miss Flite, Gridley, or Rick? The novel makes sufficiently clear there is only one possible answer: that ruin itself is what they are seeking. What else *could* they be seeking in such a place? As this pathological pattern emerges the court comes increasingly to represent, as the Marshalsea does in *Little Dorrit,* not a mere iniquitous institution like the magistrate's court in *Oliver Twist* or the Yorkshire schools in *Nicholas Nickleby,* but a comprehensive image of a factor in modern life whose vast scope and significance Dickens is among the first to diagnose so lucidly: the neurotic impulse to self-destruction. This impulse takes its plainest form among the suitors of Chancery, perhaps, but it proves (in increasingly subtle variations) to be widespread among other *Bleak House* characters as well, such as Trooper George, morbidly content to hang for a murder he did not commit, the angelic Ada Clare, whose gravitation toward the doomed Rick

Carstone hints that ruin has attractions for her, too, or even John Jarndyce, whose hysterical running away to avoid being thanked has strongly self-destructive overtones. In fact, few of the sympathetic characters of this novel are free of this kind of neurotic impulse; it assumes the proportions of another, more mysterious form of epidemic.

In the course of *Bleak House* Dickens elaborately analyzes the forms of neurosis, and his terms strikingly prefigure Freud's conception of a state of groundless guilt that, since no amount of virtuous conduct can possibly expunge it, "expresses itself as a need for punishment." In the context of puritanical Victorian culture, Dickens implies, a disposition to moral goodness almost necessarily implies a proneness to debilitating guilty anxieties. This is certainly the case, for example, of the good-natured Mr. Snagsby, whose half-comic story epitomizes the neurotic pattern and its connection with Dickens's gothic romance. Snagsby finds himself haunted by the suspicions of his harridan wife and, apparently, of Tulkinghorn, that he has somehow been up to no good; and although he knows himself to be in fact entirely blameless he is assaulted fantastically by a "hangdog sense of guilt" so acute that he is driven by it almost to the verge of insanity.

The full eeriness of this mental state is imaged in the figure of Mrs. Snagsby, who metamorphoses herself into another *Bleak House* specter, this one a pure mental apparition. To the agonized man under her surveillance she seems to swell into a supernatural pursuer, "a ghostly shade," "shadow of his shadow." In his haunted mood Snagsby begins to yearn for some cleansing punishment. "His mental sufferings are so great," explains the narrator, "that he entertains wandering ideas of delivering himself up to justice, and requiring to be cleared, if innocent, and punished with the utmost rigour of the law, if guilty." The derangement that Dickens diagnoses so matter-of-factly represents, we can see, one more emergence of the theme of "unreal things"—here, Snagsby's non-existent guilt, which even he comes to believe in—assuming real power; hence its persistent association with ghostly mystery. Snagsby's case also serves to gloss a number of equivalent ones in which the sensation of guilt is projected imagistically in the same terms of gothic occultism. Inspector Bucket, for example, regularly appears to his victims not as a flesh-and-blood police officer but as a "hovering" omniscient spy who can inspire terror "with one ghostly beat of his forefinger in the air" and who possesses "a ghostly manner of appearing" out of thin air to apprehend the guilty. In the same way Lady Dedlock's obsessive sense of guilt also appears to spring diabolically to life and to attack her in the shape of a terrible, accusing, quasi-supernatural bogey, Tulkinghorn. Of all the novel's studies of the occult projections of guilt, however, none is more elaborately conceived than the story of Esther Summerson, the most explicit case history in Dickens's fiction of the subtle link between moral virtue and mental pathology.

Esther's is a life mysteriously begun, as her aunt declares, in a phrase that brings to mind all the phantasmal presences of this novel, "with . . . a shadow on it." Esther's shadow in the first instance is her illegitimacy, which fills her, as her aunt's fanatically Calvinistic teaching ensures, with the sensation, as mysterious as the appeal of Chancery, of causeless guilt. Dickens's stress on the uncanniness of this state could not be stronger. Esther thus vows to try, she says, "as hard as ever I could, to repair the fault I had been born with (of which I confusedly felt guilty and yet innocent)." From Esther's point of view her eerie physical resemblance to her long-lost mother comes as a confirmation of her own deeply internalized neurosis. When she discovers it she is filled with the sensation of renewed guilt, and as though to rationalize this phenomenon to herself she blames herself for being the innocent cause of exposing her mother to persecution; but unconsciously their resemblance is charged with deeper psychic significance than this. It is from Esther's point of view an occult emblem of her actually inheriting, just as her aunt's original-sin theology stipulated, her mother's sexual guilt. "I felt," Esther says, "as if the blame and the shame were all in me, and the visitation had come down." This magical (that is, pathological) transfer of guilt has an uncanniness that is entirely in keeping with the large argument of *Bleak House* and that is made explicit in the episode of Esther's nocturnal visit to Chesney Wold. She finds herself prowling along the Ghost's Walk, and in a moment of hallucinatory panic that fills her, she says, with "a terror of myself," undergoes another fantastic transfer: she recognizes *herself* as the ghastly Dedlock specter, the very image of guilt and disgrace. This moment brings home to the reader, if the point had not been clear before, that the far-fetched "romantic" story of the Ghost's Walk and its sinister apparition is just an allegory of what Dickens presents as the most "familiar," or at least the most pervasive, mental state of the age, and a key to its chronic mood of fear, the susceptibility to neurotic guilt. The persistence with which Dickens links neurosis and virtue, as though the former were almost a necessary concomitant of the latter, makes the moral argument of *Bleak House* a deeply problematical one.

In the novel's ghost-haunted fables of guilt, therefore, the gothic terrors associated elsewhere in the story with the public world and its hidden systems of poverty, neglect, and exploitation are found to be congruent with the endemic *mental* systems of this culture. Social and psychological structures in *Bleak House* are reflexes of each other. What is finally implied here, as I have suggested already, is an idea that contemporary institutions, alien and merely predatory as they seem, are subtly in *sympathy* with—indeed are built upon—the mental states of their victims. Such a speculation sheds light on the cases of Chancery suitors like Rick, Miss Flite, and Gridley: are they and their countless fellow victims of the court, like Joseph K. in *The Trial,* simply delivering themselves up to justice, and to inevitable condemnation, from some haunting idea that this is just what they deserve after all? Carrying the point further, the principle suggested above helps to make sense of the great riddle implied by the "topical" side of *Bleak House:* the riddle of why England continues to tolerate all the obvious lethal disorders of contemporary life: poverty, contagion, worse-than-useless public institutions, and so forth. Dickens suggests the profound insight that there is finally no rational answer to this question, only the irrational one offered by Miss Flite with regard to Chancery but widely applicable, if we make the leap of thought that Dickens's fiction invites, to other abuses: that somehow "there's a dreadful attraction" in them, that they arise and ramify themselves in mysterious response to the self-destructive pathology that lies at the heart of this puritanical, guilt-ridden culture. The progressive coming into focus of this thesis throughout *Bleak House* gives the idea of "the romantic side of familiar things"— the idea, that is, of occult forces secretly pervading ordinary life—its widest significance of all.

III

The argument that we are tracing has at least one more major facet, in which Dickens gives a vision of the ultimate fate of personality in the quasi-occult environment of the present day. The essence of this vision is dramatized in the story of Rick Carstone, who by dint of haunting the mazes of the "horrible phantom," of "fighting with shadows and being defeated by them," steadily fades away into a pale, haggard, guilt-ridden ghost of the person he once was: he becomes, as he himself puts it, "a poor stray shadow," "quite destitute of colour." In the root sense of the word, the sense sharply underlined by Miss Flite's image of the Chancery devils relentlessly drawing personality out of their victims, Rick is *exhausted;* and in this state he becomes yet a new kind of *Bleak House* "shadow." Gridley suffers just the same fate: "His voice had faded, with the old expression of his face, with his strength, with his anger, with his resistance. . . . The faintest shadow of an object full of form and colour, is such a picture of it, as he was of the man from Shropshire whom we had spoken with before." The macabre process of dissolution repeats itself often in the ghostly, depleted victims encountered throughout the novel: in the ghosts of past victims of Chancery—Tom Jarndyce, say—who seem to hover on the peripheries of the story, in the phantasmal woman whom Esther glimpses as she commits suicide in the river, "a shadowy . . . figure that flitted past," and especially, as we have seen, in the swarming denizens of Tom-all-Alone's, whom Dickens pictures as shades in a tormented underworld, "flitting, and whistling, and skulking about." As the above examples suggest, Dickens portrays this eerie metamorphosis with the kind of obsessive insistence that is the hallmark of *Bleak House*. His most sustained studies of the transformation, however, lie in his treatments of Captain Hawdon (who takes the name Nemo after fading away so drastically as to become in his own mind "no one") and of his one-time mistress Lady Dedlock. I want in closing this essay to focus briefly on these two figures.

Nemo is one of Dickens's most compelling fictional creations, and from one point of view, if it does not sound frivolous to say so, can be regarded almost as the story's central character: this although we never hear him say a word (except a phrase or two by hearsay) and only catch one glimpse of him—as a corpse in a darkened room. It is this tantalizing half-unreality that Dickens, exploring yet again the *idée fixe* of the novel, and executing at the same time a brilliant narrative conceit, makes the center of the character. Like Esther, Nemo returns amazingly from the dead, but only in spectral, depleted form; then he vanishes again almost as the novel begins. Michael Ragussis has precisely described this effect. Nemo, he says, "is dead before the reader . . . ever gets to see him: he enters the

novel as a ghost, already dead." All that remains from the evapora-
tion of his dashing original self is the residue formed by those few
tangible shreds and traces by which he is tirelessly sought throughout the novel: the distinctive handwriting that Lady Dedlock recognizes on the Chancery affidavits; the small notice advertising "a
respectable man aged forty-five" available for copying; his signature
on the bills held by Grandfather Smallweed; the scrap of his writing
kept as a cherished souvenir by his old subaltern and friend Trooper
George. Dickens plays richly on this idea of Nemo's dissolution into
these last material traces, which amounts to a realistic version of the
process represented fantastically in Krook's macabre combustion.

On rereading the novel, when one is aware of the influence
which Nemo has exercised and will continue to exercise upon the
lives of nearly every important character in the story, it is possible to
appreciate what a powerful artistic effect Dickens contrives in the
early chapters by taking the reader so near him—Esther at one point
pauses outside Nemo's closed door—and never vouchsafing a single
glimpse of him. Dickens will not allow the shadowy law-writer to
appear in the flesh, and we are given as a result the poignant sense of
an invisible, intangible figure hovering in limbo just outside our field
of vision, having dwindled to such a ghostly state that he can no
longer emerge into the substantial world. When we finally get our
one brief glimpse of Nemo as a ragged, yellowish corpse in "spectral
darkness" whose "track" through life seems to have become unre-
coverable, he is the very image of that total unravelling of the self
that is so often witnessed in *Bleak House* and so intimately associated
with the novel's motifs of gothic horror. Only at this point does
Nemo begin in weird ways to extend his influence and to regain
much of the distinctness of form which he had seemingly lost for
good. When Jo eulogizes him in chapter 11, praising his kindness,
the ragged corpse in bare feet begins for the first time to take on a
shadowy human outline, as though returning from the dead all over
again. As the story unfolds we discover that the dead man has had
similar effects on other people, for both Honoria Dedlock and George
Rouncewell still cherish his memory and risk calamity for his sake.
Dead as he was twice certified to be, and wrapped in obscurity as he
remains, it thus becomes clear, thanks to his continuing hold upon
the living, that Hawdon/Nemo still enjoys a kind of life. But although he pervades the tale he can never escape his limbo of unseen

half-unreality—and his crepuscular reappearance in Lady Dedlock's life only unleashes disastrous consequences for one and all.

As for Lady Dedlock, her suppression of her original identity has proved all too effective and has turned her into yet another image of ghostly "exhaustion." As she puts it, she is "bored to death." In this state of death-in-life she has none of the blazing charm that similarly artificial characters have, say, for Proust. Her considerable poignancy as a fictional being arises instead from the aura of phantasmal unreality with which the subtly textured prose of *Bleak House* persistently invests her. We have the impression of always seeing her from a great distance, as though through the eyes of the Fashionable Intelligence which hazily follows her progress from place to place: or rather, we never quite seem to see her at all, even when she is there before our eyes. A typical moment is the description of her supposedly glamorous portrait in Jobling's Galaxy Gallery of British Beauty, "in which she is represented on a terrace, with a pedestal upon the terrace, and a vase upon the pedestal, and her shawl upon the vase, and a prodigious piece of fur upon the shawl, and her arm on the prodigious piece of fur, and a bracelet on her arm." What is striking, of course, is that Lady Dedlock is not recognizably there at all, except for that seemingly dismembered arm piled up with all the other inert jumble of objects. The effect is deliberately a macabre and fantastic one, and suggests that Lady Dedlock too has suffered a recession into the domain of phantomlike shadows.

The suggestion is constantly underscored, as, for example, at the moment when she appears before Guppy in her library. "Presently he hears a rustling. Is it—? No, it's no ghost; but fair flesh and blood, most brilliantly dressed." This description, or rather nondescription, is all that we get of her on this occasion, and again it is the entire blankness of visual detail that is striking, and that suggests perhaps that it may be a ghost after all. At other times Lady Dedlock seems to exist only as an eerily disembodied voice, as in the half-phantasmagorical scene in the keeper's lodge where she seems, hidden as she is in the shadows, to speak out of thin air, giving Esther the impression of hearing a voice transmitted uncannily from her distant past. Thus Dickens constantly suggests, with a wealth of finely-conceived imagery, Lady Dedlock's attenuation into a shadowy and unreal figure. This is exactly the doom acted out climactically in the episode of her suicidal flight at the end. She vanishes altogether from the scene as Dickens removes us to the point of view of her pursuers, Esther and Bucket, and by this device vividly accents that quality of attenuation and illusoriness that has surrounded Lady Dedlock all along, here swallowing her up once and for all. She seems to dissolve into thin air. Like Hawdon, she is thus reduced at last to "no one," and friends who strive to reclaim her find that they can only pursue her at a great distance, occasionally getting fragmentary clues to her existence through scraps of writing left behind or reports that filter back from the darkness through word of mouth. The eeriness of this effect is highlighted by an important device that has been described by Taylor Stoehr: that of surrounding Lady Dedlock with *Doppelgängers* like Mademoiselle Hortense, Esther, and Jenny the brickmaker's wife, figures who seem like quasi-magical refractions or projections of aspects of her own self. Her story, on one level a fable of the haunting destructiveness of guilt, is on another, as these doublings and triplings suggest, a fable of psychological disintegration of such a drastic and arcane kind that it can only be evoked by intimations of supernatural mystery.

The important parallelism between the careers of Nemo and Lady Dedlock lies, then, in their suffering the same fate of being transformed at last into ghostly shadows—and thus of illustrating in climactic form the syndromes of psychic deterioration that are rampant in the world of *Bleak House* and everywhere linked, as we have seen, to hints of the occult. These lines of Dickens's story epitomize his fundamental scheme, with its deeply embedded lesson in literary history, of revealing the conventional devices of gothic horror-romance not as mere elements of fantasy but as prime metaphors of life in the alienating world of "the central streets of any great modern city." What these metaphors steadily project, as we have seen, is the sensation of hallucinatory strangeness and the suppressed, almost subliminal current of panic that modern cities generate, conditions that Dickens traces to the influence of a constellation of insidious "unreal things" that have come to usurp tangible realities and increasingly to govern the texture of everyday life. These influences are both the causes and the symptoms of the deeply altered, and deeply pathological, state of consciousness that forms the central subject of *Bleak House*.

The leading quality of the argument that we have sketched is the way it boldly correlates such a wide range of seemingly disparate phenomena. The invisibility of stark urban poverty, the sinister complexities of public institutions, an epidemic of neurosis, strange evaporations of selfhood: all these diverse aspects of contemporary experience are powerfully linked together in *Bleak House* in an indivisible complex, treated in effect as cognate manifestations of some underlying principle that itself remains enigmatic. This, if anything, is the "sinister, supernatural agency" that one senses hovering over the story. But there is nothing at all superstitious about *Bleak House;* Dickens uses gothic fantasy—the point is worth repeating—as a means of transcribing factors in the contemporary environment that almost by definition must elude ordinary realism (being, as they are, "unreal things"). More than this, "the romantic side" of *Bleak House* strongly suggests the capacity of metaphor to operate not just as a means of transcription but as an active instrument of discovery and understanding. The ramifying theme of occult haunting in this novel performs for all its trivial origins much the same sequence of functions that the theoretician of science Thomas S. Kuhn attributes to a revolutionary "paradigm" in scientific research. First, he says, the new paradigm causes an array of unnoticed phenomena to leap into prominence and call urgently for interpretation; then it is the means of linking them together in an integrated pattern that amounts to a new vision of the world—or a new world, period. As Kuhn puts it, in language immediately reminiscent of Dickens's preface, the formulation of a compelling new paradigm enlarges scientific understanding by causing "familiar objects [to be] seen in a different light" and thus to reveal unsuspected properties and interrelations. What I have proposed as the central paradigm of *Bleak House,* the idea of the contemporary scene as a field of occult forces, retrains our vision on familiar things in just this way and produces an amazingly rich yield of insights into the workings and interworkings of both the social and the mental worlds. The logic of Dickens's large scheme remains for the most part intuitive, elliptical, and metaphorical, although the more one thinks about it the more it promises to make profound sense that, say, the age of invisible poverty should coincide with the age of neurotic guilt and also, in another sphere, of madly disordered courts of law. To an extent rarely met in novels, this impulse to understand the connections of large systems of phenomena is central to the imagination of *Bleak House;* and what governs this impulse at every point, as I have tried to show, is Dickens's intuition that beneath the surface of "familiar things" in modern England lies a maelstrom of occult apparitions.

Double Vision and the Double Standard in *Bleak House:* A Feminist Perspective

Virginia Blain

The device of dual narration has often been taken to be the key to interpreting *Bleak House,* but I should like to suggest that previous discussions have overlooked an important aspect of Dickens's use of this device. It seems to me that the juxtaposition of the two narrative voices sets up a submerged dialectic between male and female viewpoints, and that once we are aware of the operation of this dialectic, other features of the novel take on a new significance. John Carey has drawn attention to the way in which suppressed violence can give rise to sexual conflict in Dickens's novels. Such conflict, I would suggest, informs not only the vision of violence in familial and personal relationships in *Bleak House,* but also the vision of hidden violence in the legal system. I draw on the work of René Girard in support of my perception of the significance of this link between the legal and the social/sexual bases of society as portrayed in *Bleak House.* The proposition Girard puts to us about the hidden connections in a modern society between violence and sexuality appears to be unconsciously sensed by Dickens. Dickens's perception of the gender division into "separate spheres" for men and women affords him the opportunity for a dual viewpoint on societal corruption, both public and private. But through its articulation as a dialectic the narrative structure does more than this, in my view. Its workings produce a novel which probes deeply at the roots of this corruption and strongly suggests that they are at least partly embedded in the violence of hidden sexual hostilities. The text thus carries inscribed

From *Literature and History* 11, no. 1 (Spring 1985). © 1985 by Thames Polytechnic.

within it a significance for a late twentieth-century female reader, in particular, which it did not reveal to earlier critics or to the author himself.

In part I of the discussion which follows, I aim to give an understanding of the importance of the male/female dialectic both to the structure of the novel and, more particularly, to the characterization of Esther. In parts II and III, where the focus shifts onto Esther's mother, I shall point to some hitherto unrecognized aspects of Lady Dedlock's pivotal role in the novel. I also offer a new interpretation of her relationship with the legally established patriarchy (especially Mr Tulkinghorn) on the one hand, and with her illegitimate daughter, Esther, on the other. Finally, in part IV, I shall suggest that her chase and death take on a new significance when they are read as part of a purification rite for a whole diseased society.

I

Dickens's use in *Bleak House* of the unusual strategy of dual narration has drawn from his commentators no mean portion of the critical debate which surrounds this novel. The role of Esther Summerson has long been a major focus for controversy, and in recent years a great deal of energy has been expended on what one critic has called "the rehabilitation of Esther Summerson." The case for the psychological "truth" of her presentation as a young woman of some emotional retardation, springing from an early childhood deprived of love and esteem, and warped by her inturned sense of social guilt, has been sufficiently well-documented to need no further elaboration here. The omniscient narrator, in his turn, has been subjected to various modes of critical investigation, though not under quite the same cloud of controversy that has shadowed discussion of Esther. Although few since E. M. Forster (in *Aspects of the Novel*) have wanted to argue that this narrative voice is that of Dickens himself, equally few have dared to follow Grahame Smith's example, in his monograph of *Bleak House* (London, 1974), in proffering a full identikit portrait of this protean figure:

> The narrator of *Bleak House* is an educated man, but not one who feels the need to make a display of his learning, and this is part of a general pattern of characteristics that I would suggest make the narrator a coherent figure. . . . I see the third-person narrator of *Bleak House* as urbane,

witty, cultured; in short a man of the world, but a man of
the world whose poise never degenerates into cynicism.

Nonetheless, even among those who take up neither of these
extreme positions, there is one point of unspoken agreement: that of
the omniscient narrator's gender. He is unquestionably male. Even if
he is nothing but a voice, it is a male voice. This seems to me to be
one of those points which are so obvious that their significance is in
danger of being missed; but when we remind ourselves on whose
vision the idea of omniscience is ultimately based ("Our *Father*" of
Jo's dying prayer) we perceive afresh some of the assumptions we
have been used to making about Victorian literature. An omniscient
narrator was masculine almost by definition. To my knowledge,
there was no model of female omniscience available to Victorian
novelists, either in literature or in heaven.

I want to argue that it has a profound significance for the meaning of *Bleak House* as a whole when we read it as a novel told half
from a male standpoint and half from a female. In earlier studies, the
differences between the two narrating voices in *Bleak House* have
been accounted for in different ways by different critics. Esther's is
the "inner" voice, his the "outer" voice; hers is the subjective voice,
his the objective; hers is personal, his impersonal. Each of these
qualities can of course be seen as glosses on the basic premise that one
voice is feminine and one is masculine. The inner perspective, the
subjective viewpoint, the interest bounded by personal limits, these
are all qualities typically, even archetypically, associated with the
feminine principle, while objectivity, impersonality and largeness of
vision all belong to the masculine realm.

The full significance of Esther Summerson's "femaleness," in
her narrator's role and in the action, has yet to be charted. Ellen
Moers has called it "the single 'women question' novel in the Dickens
canon," and it certainly seems clear that in this novel Dickens had a
great many things he wanted to say about women and their social
and sexual roles. In order to say them convincingly, he hit upon the
brilliant idea of presenting one woman's experience of herself and of
womanhood as part of the reader's very means of vision, part of the
experience of reading the novel. Twentieth-century readers might
wish to object that Esther, as "female eunuch" *par excellence,* is dis-
qualified from speaking authoritatively of or from female experience. But this argument can be reversed very easily when we

remember how pervasive in the middle classes was the notion of women as "relative creatures" at this period in Queen Victoria's reign: creatures destined solely to be a man's helpmate, as daughter, wife, or mother, for whom any separate individual identity was seen to be a burden. Thus Esther, far from being an unrepresentative woman, might well be seen as archetypically representative of the Victorian middle-class woman who has been shaped by her adoption of the values of the patriarchal society she inhabits, and whose own selfhood is very much in question as a result.

It is important to emphasize the structural significance of Dickens's choice of a female narrative voice as a counterbalance to the masculine omniscient narrator. Each has been given almost exactly half the space of the novel. While the masculine, all-knowing voice offers us the analytical overview of the novel's world, the viewpoint (to adapt Hillis Miller's definition of the omniscient narrator's role) of the middle class male community mind becomes aware of itself; the female, limited voice, by contrast, gives us the private, personal viewpoint. Esther cannot tell about either the working of the law in Chancery, or the making of the law in Parliament; as a woman, she is shut out from these two patriarchal structures, and as an illegitimate woman she is placed at an even further remove from the centre of legal power. Thus, paradoxically her "inner" view of characters and events is really that of an outsider in society, while the other narrator's "outer" view springs very much from an inside vantage point.

Although many of the same characters appear in each, the two narratives are not alternative accounts of the same events. Of course, by choosing Esther to offset his omniscient narrator, Dickens is able to reinforce not only the separation between the male and female viewpoint, by allowing to each a particular sphere of comment, but also their difference, which he exploits by using each as a purveyor of criticism of the other's domain. Some of this criticism is explicit (and can therefore be read as consciously intended), but a more subversive criticism is inscribed implicitly within the text. In making what might at first seem a perverse allocation of material, and giving the telling of the story of Richard Carstone's battle with Chancery to the female narrative voice and the story of Lady Dedlock's guilty secret to the male narrative voice, the novel is opening a pathway for a commentary on the male preserve of legal inheritance from a female standpoint, and on the female "preserve" of illicit sexuality

(Lady Dedlock) or illegal inheritance (Esther herself)—from a male. For Esther's narration gives no glow of feminine (or sentimental) sympathy to Richard's story; as Taylor Stoehr rightly points out, she in fact makes a less than sympathetic narrator of this tale of failure and suffering. Equally or even more surely, the detached voice of the omniscient narrator, with his relentlessly rhetorical insistence on the allegory of the Ghost's Walk, succeeds in achieving an almost total alienation of the most sympathetic reader from the plight of the unhappy Lady Dedlock.

II

Lady Dedlock's melodramatic tale of woe has indeed often been regarded as an unfortunate intrusion in the novel, an instance of Dickens's inability to sustain a wholly unified concept of the novel as artistic structure. In my reading however, Lady Dedlock is vital to the balance of the whole novel, and at least as crucial a figure as the Lord Chancellor himself (in both his manifestations). Dickens points similarities between the latter's Court of Chancery and Lady Dedlock's world of fashion (both "things of precedent and usage") as early as chapter 2, and it is clear that she is as powerful a figurehead in the hierarchy of the female world as he is in the male. Further, both are dependent finally upon the power of parliamentary law, resting at this time largely in the hands of the aristocracy, represented in the novel by Sir Leicester Dedlock. To Sir Leicester's fellows and their hereditary power, the Lord Chancellor owes his position, and to Sir Leicester himself, and the hereditary station he occupies, Lady Dedlock owes hers. "Indeed, he married her for love. A whisper still goes about, that she had not even family."

The comparison between the structural function of these two pivotal figures can be carried further and by implication can be seen to mirror the structural function of the two narrative voices. The Lord Chancellor's Quilpish double, "lord chancellor" Krook, subsumes into himself all the smouldering violence which can find no outlet in the real Court of Chancery, thus freeing the true Lord Chancellor to appear "both courtly and kind" (Esther's words in chap. 3). Similarly, Lady Dedlock has a double or surrogate, no less sinister in kind than Krook. This of course is the Frenchwoman Hortense, perceived in a striking passage in chapter 18 as deliberately walking shoeless through the wet grass "as if through blood," and who, like Krook, has the function of drawing to herself much of the passionate violence that one might have expected to accrue to a woman in Lady Dedlock's increasingly beseiged position as she engages more and more fully in her secret and deadly duel with Tulkinghorn.

Then again, there is a strong parallel between the Lord Chancellor and Lady Dedlock in their relative positions as parent figures: "The Lord High Chancellor, at his best, appeared so poor a substitute for the love and pride of parents," muses Esther (chap. 3), but does she convince us that she holds any better an opinion of her own mother? "I told her . . . [t]hat it was not for me, then resting *for the first time,* on my mother's bosom, to take her to account for having given me life" (chap. 36, my italics). Both the Lord Chancellor, *in loco parentis* to Richard and Ada, and Lady Dedlock, aided to ignorance of her child's need by her barbarous sister, are well-intentioned in theory but profoundly damaging in practice towards their children. It is no accident that we are shown mad Miss Flite deluded into inventing an unhappy marriage between Lady Dedlock and the Lord Chancellor: "in *my* opinion . . . she's the Lord Chancellor's wife. He's married, you know. And I understand she leads him a terrible life" (chap. 35).

It is surely not surprising that we can trace such parallels as these in *Bleak House.* That the novel achieves its effects largely by the exploitation of parallels and hidden connections has long been recognised. What *is* perhaps surprising is that critics have continued to puzzle over what has been called the "problem" of the novel's having two "centres," the Chancery centre and the Lady Dedlock centre. Even Hillis Miller, who assures us in his introduction to the Penguin edition (1971) that:

> Metaphor and metonymy together make up the deep grammatical armature by which the reader of *Bleak House* is led to make a whole out of discontinuous parts

is obliged to admit the possibility that Angus Wilson was right in seeing the double centre as a fault in the novel. Miller writes:

> The most salient case of an apparent loose end or inconsistency is the failure to integrate perfectly the two major plots. This fissure in the novel, a conspicuous rift in its web, seems all the more inexplicable when we consider

Dickens's obvious care in other parts of the book to tie together apparently unrelated details. . . . Surely, the reader supposes, Dickens could have related Lady Dedlock's "crime" more closely to the corrupting effect of Chancery if he had wanted to do so. Perhaps he did not want to. Perhaps he wanted to mislead the reader into thinking that the revelation of Lady Dedlock's secret is at the same time an explanation of the real mystery of the novel—that is, the question of why English society is in such a sad state?

"Mislead" Hillis Miller might think it does, but is this not a twentieth-century critic's misreading of what Dickens would have seen merely as a question of "leading"? He has so often been accused of unconscious sexism (as though a man of his time and background could *not* have been sexist—unless or even if he were John Stuart Mill) that we may have blinded ourselves to the possibility that by the very fact of his being *more* aware of the distinction between male and female roles in society, his "sexism" was at least less unconscious than that of his twentieth-century critics. Miller is pursuing other goals in his essay, and ignores what perhaps seems to him too simple an interpretation to be a key to the connection between Lady Dedlock and her secret life, and the world of the Lord High Chancellor. Yet surely there are grounds for suggesting that one is a symptomatic representative of the novel's women, and the other, of the novel's men? A reading along these lines would put the vexed question of the division between the sexes near the heart of the novel's meaning.

Despite the recognition critics like Butt and Tillotson have given to the importance of the satire of women in the novel, despite the recognition that half the novel has been "handed over" to a female narrator, it is remarkable that no one has argued that the key to the relationship between the "two centres" is precisely the relationship between the sexes. That Dickens should have chosen Lady Dedlock and her illegitimate daughter as representative examples of the female sex is both extraordinary and profoundly significant; and it is equally significant, though less immediately extraordinary, that he chose lawyers for his "representative" males. For the whole legal system sustaining Chancery is in its very essence a man's preserve, where lawyers inherit causes from their fathers, where the male mystique is as powerful as, if more sinister than, that surrounding a privileged gentlemen's club. Not only do Chancery lawyers inherit causes through the male line; they also control the pattern of property inheritance within a whole society, ensuring the continuance of patriarchy.

If it is true, as has often been claimed, that Chancery acts as a moral yardstick for characters in the novel, then Dickens must be assumed to be aware that it effectively excludes almost all the female characters from its particular challenge, since they have little or no place in the struggle over inherited property which, by the law itself, generally belonged to their "legal" representative, man. Lady Dedlock, ironically enough, has brought as her only "dowry" to Sir Leicester her interest in the Jarndyce case; Ada forfeits her property rights to Richard upon marriage (and indeed he then spends—or borrows against—her expectations as well as his own); only the unattached Miss Flite finds a regular (or irregular) place in court entirely of her own account; and of course, it sends her mad. But the fact that Chancery is an inapposite moral testing device for women in the novel does not mean that Dickens has left them unprovided for. Their touchstone is the highly charged symbol of the hearth and home. Just as it is lamentably easy for men to make a Bleak House of the Court of Chancery or of Tom-all-Alone's, so it is all too easy for women to make a Bleak House of a home (only Esther being supremely gifted with the opposite ability). I want now to examine some of the ways in which the novel develops this theme.

Lady Dedlock is the paradigm for all the failed homemakers in the novel. We are early forewarned of her "hearth-rending" propensities, and she is indeed the stereotype of the fallen woman, for whom redemption within a Victorian novel was next to impossible. But in developing links of identity between Lady Dedlock and other female characters such as Hortense, Jenny (whose clothes she dons for death), and of course Esther herself (whose *alter ego* she increasingly becomes), the novel gives credence to the notion of a secret community among women, and further contrives to hint that a society which tolerates such a woman as Lady Dedlock as one of its chief representatives of womanhood will find her taint spreading to all members of the sex, just as the taint of Chancery defiles all men who touch it. In one sense, Dickens was certainly concerned to keep the two plots separate. Like Ruskin, for whom *Bleak House* might well have stood as a source, Dickens apparently believed in the separate realms of "Kings' Treasuries" and "Queens' Gardens," and he could never have intended, as one of his recent critics argues, that Esther should be regarded, not as a woman, but as a "sexually undifferentiated hero."

There is no evidence in this novel to show that Dickens wanted any real integration of man's and woman's worlds. Even those female characters who exhibit "manly" qualities of leadership and strength without apparently forfeiting authorial approval (Mrs Bagnet, Mrs Bucket, Mrs Rouncewell) are still shown to be putting the interests of husband or son before their own. Woman, ideally at least, is the upholder of the private inner world of the family, the keeper of the sanctity of the hearth and, most importantly of all, the guardian of chastity; while man is the upholder of the public outer world of the "family" of England, and governor and the guardian of the law. Dickens sets up numerous analogies and parallels between these roles or spheres and between the corruptions each is heir to, but there seems little point in criticising him for "failure" to integrate the Chancery and Lady Dedlock plots when one of his chief objects appears to be to keep them apart, both in theory and in practice, the better to serve as comments on, and parallels to, each other. For the gender division as Dickens saw it offered an opportunity for a split viewpoint not only on society's rotting superstructure of legal, aristocratic, hereditary privilege, but also on the hidden source of this corruption—the underlying propensity to violence.

III

Every community in so-called civilized societies contains repressed violence. After all, it is the fear of community hostility and disorder breaking into open acts of violence which has led to the establishment of judicial systems to control man's litigious nature. Under a judicial system, as René Girard argues in his seminal work *Violence and the Sacred,* vengeance is rationalized, and unlike the individual, this system "never hesitates to confront violence head on, because it possesses a monopoly on the means of revenge." In this regard, as Girard makes plain, modern societies are not so far removed as they might like to think from primitive communities where the ritual sacrifice of a surrogate victim or scapegoat serves as a purgation of violence by metamorphosing the very real (though often hidden) hostilities that all members of a community feel for one another into a common hostility against an object chosen precisely because of its inability to avenge itself. Like the primitive urge to find a sacrificial victim, the law contains in its own ritualised actions the violence it seeks to quell.

This is why there is so much mythic resonance to be found in the placing of Chancery and the figure of Lady Dedlock within the same novel. Sexuality, as Girard reminds us, "is a permanent source of disorder even within the most harmonious of communities . . . [it] leads to quarrels, jealous rages, mortal combats." Social guilt and social violence are openly examined in the novel: sexual guilt and sexual violence run like a hidden stream beneath. John Carey is surely right to insist that "violence and destruction were the most powerful stimulants to [Dickens's] imagination." One of Dickens's great achievements in *Bleak House,* it seems to me, lies in giving such evocative expression to a fear that society's controls over violence in the community are breaking down, so that the very institutions designed to offer most protection to individuals—Chancery or the Law on the one hand, the Family on the other and, underpinning both, Religion itself—are being subverted into instruments of the very violence which is such a threat to social order.

The attention that has been directed by so many critics to the platitudinous side of the novel, to the notion that Dickens recommended as solution to the corrupt state of England a more thorough and dutiful housekeeping, so that the cosy warmth of Esther in Bleak House might be writ large throughout the commonwealth, has drawn notice away from those parts of the book which speak to us so much more profoundly because they are animated by so much more creative energy. In allowing the character of Lady Dedlock to serve as scapegoat for the sexual and ultimately, I would contend, the social ills of society, Dickens not only shows us how a male-dominated system will always find a way to let its men both eat their cake and have it—indulge sexual appetite while condemning it—but also reveals, albeit unwittingly, something of the same propensity in himself as author. How else do we account for the submerged or guilty celebration of sexual violence which lurks about the figure of the rascally Krook and his mysterious feline companion, Lady Jane?

The telling symbol of the "marriage" imagined by mad Miss Flite as connecting the Lord Chancellor and Lady Dedlock is daringly echoed in the highly suggestive portrayal of the relationship between the bottle shop Lord Chancellor Krook, with his "three sacks of ladies' hair below," and Lady Jane.

"Hi, Lady Jane!"

A large grey cat leapt . . . on his shoulder and startled us all.

"Hi! show 'em how you scratch. Hi! Tear, my lady!" said her master.

The cat leaped down, and ripped at a bundle of rags with her tigerish claws, with a sound that it set my teeth on edge to hear.

(chap. 5)

Compare this to the description of Hortense mastered by Bucket in chapter 54:

"I would like to kiss her!" exclaims Mademoiselle Hortense panting tigress-like.

"You'd bite her, I suspect," says Mr Bucket.

"I would!" making her eyes very large.

"I would love to tear her, limb from limb."

I cannot believe it an accident that Krook's sinister cat, with her witch-like propensity for feasting on corpses (after being ejected from the dead Nemo's room, "she goes furtively downstairs winding her lithe tail and licking her lips") and with her association by imagery with the tigerish Hortense, should have been given an aristocratic name that allows Krook to address her as "My Lady." These associations link her immediately with Lady Dedlock, and suggest further, a titillating combination of childlike purity and corrupt sexuality. Being a grey cat, she was probably named after the unfortunate Lady Jane Grey, described by Dickens in his *Child's History* as: "amiable, learned, and clever," "young . . . innocent and fair," who only accepted the crown "in obedience to her father and mother." At the same time, the vulgar sense of "Lady Jane" as a name for the female genitals familiar to the modern reader from Lawrence's *Lady Chatterley's Lover* is recorded in Partridge as being in popular use from at least 1850. Thus Lady Jane offers, by her very name, a fitting double image of the female sex, and reinforces the suggestion, already implicit in Hortense, that beneath Lady Dedlock's frozen surface lurks fiendish powers of destruction, if once "the floodgates were opened," to use Sir Leicester's own words.

It is very fitting, too, that it is Krook and Lady Jane who unwittingly harbour the secrets of inheritance that have been locked up by their counterparts, the Lord Chancellor and Lady Dedlock and, implicitly, by the author in his two narrators. The true Jarndyce will is finally discovered—ironically too late to save Richard—among Krook's rubbish. Lady Dedlock, as a woman, of course has the hidden key to the secret of Esther's illegitimate "inheritance," namely, the knowledge of Esther's true parentage; and it is her own telltale love letters to Captain Hawdon which are finally discovered, again too late, in the symbolically resonant hiding place of Lady Jane's bed (chap. 54). The splendid parodic death of Chancery in Krook's transmogrification by combustion into a "cinder of a small charred and broken log of wood sprinkled with white ashes" and "a dark grey coating on the walls and ceiling" significantly leaves the equivalently parodic embodiment of female sexuality, Krook's cat, alive and snarling at what little remains of her master.

It is the dark and sinisterly masculine figure of Mr Tulkinghorn which manages to arouse the enmity of both feline females, the cat (who "expands her wicked mouth, and snarls at him" or "spits at his rusty legs . . . swearing wrathfully") and Hortense, "That feline personage, with her lips tightly shut, and her eyes looking at him sideways"; the latter, of course, eventually justifying his hostility by unleashing her innate violence and shooting him. Various motives have been suggested for Tulkinghorn's vendetta against Lady Dedlock, but the chief complaint has been about lack of motive. Critics don't seem to want to see the motive that Dickens openly supplies him with—his irrational hatred of the female sex—let alone admit its adequacy. Yet Dickens provides in Tulkinghorn a powerful illustration of the threat misogyny poses to a humanistic vision.

> There are women enough in the world, Mr Tulkinghorn thinks—too many; they are at the bottom of all that goes wrong in it, though, for the matter of that, they create business for lawyers. What would it be to see a woman going by, even though she were going secretly? They are all secret. Mr Tulkinghorn knows that, very well.
>
> (chap. 16)

Again, he says to himself:

> These women were created to give trouble, the whole earth over. The Mistress not being enough to deal with, here's the maid now! But I will be short with *this* jade at least!
>
> (chap. 42)

Marriage, too, arouses his particular scorn, especially the Dedlock marriage, where it is almost as though he is jealous of Sir Leicester's love for Lady Dedlock, with whom he is a rival for her husband's trust.

> My experience teaches me, Lady Dedlock, that most of the people I know would do far better to leave marriage alone. It is at the bottom of three-fourths of their troubles. So I thought when Sir Leicester married, and so I always have thought since.
>
> (chap. 41)

Nice as it is that the nasty old gentleman meets his nemesis through the irrational vengeance of Lady Dedlock's surrogate self, it does not in fact do that beleaguered lady much good. For his is no sacrificial death, since he has an avenger at the ready in the shape of the irrepressible and aggressively masculine Inspector Bucket. "Duty is duty, and friendship is friendship. I never want the two to clash, if I can help it," he says, as he cheerfully arrests his friend honest George for murder (chap. 49), thus showing his unhesitating allegiance to the tough masculine ethic of the law, which has its face of vengeance hidden under rationalisation. However, Lady Dedlock has by now realised that if she is to save her daughter she must destroy herself; to legitimise Esther she must take upon herself society's hostility towards the illegitimate, and accept a view of herself as guilty woman, a role of high melodrama that she proceeds to act out with a certain masochistic flair.

A society which denies the legitimacy of female sexuality is virtually denying legitimacy to women. This is why it is such a powerful part of the novel's meaning that Esther is illegitimate. The purgation of the taint of illegitimacy becomes, in a sense, the purgation of the taint of female sexuality. Lady Dedlock is a scapegoat insofar as she represents the secret "guilt" of sexuality in every woman that must be driven out of the community so that it can be purged from the threat of its own consuming violence. According to Girard, the sacrificial victim or scapegoat for a community must always be someone who is both in a respected position and at the same time, an outsider who will have no avenger. This double role Lady Dedlock fulfills perfectly. She is at the pinnacle of fashionable female society, yet she is an imposter in the ranks of the Dedlocks. Joined with her in the role of outsider are Hortense (a foreigner), Jenny (a social outcast) and Esther (illegitimate). The novel deliberately merges the identities of these women, so that when the climactic chase comes, it draws part of its power from the feeling that Lady Dedlock has taken upon herself the sacrificial role demanded of all women but carried in her case to its extreme. Esther, we remember, is told in early childhood by her aunt Barbary, in words that echo through the book:

> Your mother, Esther, is your disgrace, and you were hers. The time will come—and soon enough—when you will understand this better, and will feel it too, *as no one save a woman can.*
>
> (chap. 3, my italics)

It is of course women, who already bear the labour of birth itself, who also bear the brunt of the man-made sin of giving "illegitimate" birth. This explains the portent of the aunt's words, which fully recognise sexual transgression as a distinctively female guilt. Once again it seems that Dickens was far more aware than his liberal-minded twentieth-century critics of the extra burden such notions of illegitimacy placed upon a female bastard. Those who claim that Esther's "femaleness" is unimportant, that what matters to Dickens in her portrayal is the study of a *child,* are missing a crucial point: that an illegitimate girl has an inherited slur against her own sexual purity that would never adhere to a boy in the same position. Similarly, when Gordon Hirsch argues that "it is too restrictive to see [Esther] exclusively as a woman. Rather, she is a child of indeterminate sex, as perhaps even the sexual ambiguity of her surname, Summer-son, implies," he reveals more of his own outlook than of Dickens's. The point about her surname "Summerson" that I would wish to stress is that it is an adopted name, not her real one. Her real name—Esther Hawdon (whore; hoyden)—carries with it the awful implication of exactly what role would have awaited Esther had she been thrown into the streets as a young girl by the sanctimonious Mrs Rachael. It is again Mrs Rachael who, later in the novel (as Mrs Chadband), informs Mr Guppy that Esther is not Esther Summerson, but Esther Hawdon (chap. 29). Esther's status in the book as one of the narrators has deflected attention from the particular brand of sexual guilt she bears. Modern readers have perhaps been too ready to accept her low self-esteem as a neurotic symptom and to underestimate the extent of her plight as an illegitimate female. In the eyes of her society, she bears a sexual taint by inheritance on the distaff side. There are many hints in the novel of the sexual stigma that she has inherited from her mother; her scarring from disease contracted through no fault of her own; the humiliation inflicted on her by Mr Guppy and Mrs Woodcourt; her Aunt's prophecy ("you will feel it, as none save a woman can"). Esther's battle to establish a respectable identity ought properly to be seen in the context of a battle against unspoken imputations against her sexual purity. This, surely, underlies the otherwise inexplicable cat-and-mouse game Jarndyce plays at the end of the novel, with the object of proving to the skeptical world (represented by Mrs. Woodcourt) Esther's "true legitimacy" (chap. 64), viz. her ability to sacrifice her own sexuality (linked with her mother) to a sense of duty to her "father." Her "father," in this instance, is Jarndyce himself, but the wider implications of her duty extend to the whole patriarchal system.

IV

The sexual taint on Esther (as Dickens shows) is bestowed on her not by her mother's act so much as by the hostility to women endemic in a patriarchal society. It is this taint which sets her invisibly apart from other women and yet at the same time makes her their archetypal representative. This is because she bears within her as a deeply-buried wound the guilt and shame that the position of women in such a society inflicts on all females to some degree. Nonetheless, her "inheritance of shame" as she aptly terms it (chap. 44), can only be expunged at the cost of her joining with the patriarchy, the world of men, of male legality and legitimacy, and to do this effectively she has to cast off her mother. And this is precisely what she does, in my reading, by joining forces with Mr Bucket in the death chase of Lady Dedlock. Readers have long felt the power of this climactic chase, while being at the same time rather at a loss to account for its resonance in a novel about Chancery. I want now to offer a reading which suggests that Dickens's unerring dramatic instincts have here a deeper basis than has hitherto been suspected. This part of the novel takes on a wider significance when we realise the importance of the submerged tensions of sexual repression and vengeance which underpin it.

That Tulkinghorn and his avenger Bucket are both agents of a judicial system which has been exposed in the novel as an instrument of vengeance, and are both at the same time so strongly identified with the masculine ethic of the society, makes them fitting accomplices in the purgation of "illicit" female sexuality through the sacrifice of Lady Dedlock along with her surrogate, Hortense. Taylor Stoehr has argued that the chief weakness of the split point of view in *Bleak House* is that the two themes (Esther's sexual-social dilemma and Richard's vocational one) are never brought into meaningful contact with each other. But in my view the ultimate effect of the split narrative is, on the contrary, finally to enforce a connection, by pressing the analogy between the separate male and female spheres until they achieve climactic union in the expulsion of Lady Dedlock, who is used very precisely, in Girard's terms, as a ritual sacrificial victim or scapegoat for the transferred hostilities within a patriarchal society.

It has often been remarked that it is in the pursuit of Lady Dedlock that the two narratives draw together. Esther in her role as female voice has always been time-bound in her narration; it is the male narrator who can command the "timeless" present tense. But now for the first time, the two narratives "coincide in their focusing of time and space at the end of chapter 56" as Stoehr reminds us. He continues:

> Bucket, who has appeared in Esther's narrative only once, is now taken into her story completely, as he and Esther rush through the countryside in pursuit of Lady Dedlock. This chapter (57) and the next but one, both told from Esther's point of view, bring us to the gates of the burial ground, which also figures in Esther's narrative now for the first time, and Lady Dedlock is thus brought into her daughter's story, and out of the present-tense narrative, for good and all. The whole sequence, in which *single* chapters from the two narratives alternate for the first time in the novel, is constructed as a joining of the points of view *in order to bring Esther and her mother together.*
>
> (my italics)

It is this conclusion that I feel constrained to question, yet it is the conclusion most commonly drawn from this part of the novel. John Lucas spells it out even more clearly in his book on Dickens, *The Melancholy Man* (London, 1970), where he writes:

Esther's narrative . . . has to do with what seem to be entirely different matters and yet all the while is moving closer to the other narrative, until there is a total fusion of the two in the *girl's reunion with the mother who has denied her.*

(my italics)

What kind of "reunion" can Esther possibly have with a dead body? The mother is not only "cold and dead" when discovered by her daughter, but also in one of those disguises which is perhaps not so much a disguise as a revelation of true identity, the clothes of that more obvious social outcast, that other "distressed, unsheltered" creature, Jenny, the brickmaker's wife, whom Esther now tellingly "recognizes" as "the mother of the dead child." For surely it is the childish Esther herself who has now "died" to her mother, in order to live again—to live "legitimately"—as a woman in that very society which has made of her mother a scapegoat to purge its own sins of violence, both sexual and social. Esther, in a sense, has to "kill" her mother within herself, in order to escape her contagion. The chase by Bucket, with the passive collusion of Esther, ostensibly to "save" Lady Dedlock, has in fact resulted in her death—since the more relentless their pursuit, the more desperate her flight, and the more inevitable her end. In fulfilling the role of surrogate victim for society's guilty violence, Lady Dedlock beautifully illustrates by her melodramatic death what Girard observes in his book to be the "fundamental identity" of "vengeance, sacrifice and legal punishment."

As Girard cogently argues, the whole notion of legitimacy has grown up in our society linked with religion as a means of containing violent impulses. Sexuality is "impure" because it has to do with violence, not the other way about, and Girard notes the possibility of "some half-suppressed desire in men to place the blame for all forms of violence on women." Sir Leicester may forgive his wife her sexual transgression (once he is paralyzed, and she at the point of death); nonetheless it is deeply necessary to the mythic shape of the novel that Lady Dedlock suffer and die, cast out from society. Her punishment must exceed her "crime" for her function as ritual victim, or scapegoat, to be fulfilled. It is only by virtue of the relative innocence of a scapegoat that it can take on the burden of others' guilts. The expulsion of the scapegoat is not only part of a purification ritual, but vital in preventing violence from escalating through reciprocated acts of vengeance.

By the very act of showing Lady Dedlock as a scapegoat figure, Dickens indicates what lay just as deep and hidden in him as any horror of female power or female sexuality: a knowledge that woman was being punished for the sins of a patriarchal society. For one of the points that the novel makes about Lady Dedlock is that, as a scapegoat, she must be far *less* guilty than the society which expurgates its own violence and purifies its shrines by encouraging her death. At some level Dickens *knows* about suppressed sexual violence, and it is this knowledge, working through the dual viewpoint of the two narrators, that provides the impetus for the expulsion of Lady Dedlock when the double narrative is brought together. By implication, it is fear of the destructive power of this violence which reinforces the "separate spheres" policy of this society and which gives such a fierce edge to the novel's satire of women like Mrs Jellyby, Mrs Pardiggle and Mrs Snagsby, who try to usurp male prerogatives.

In the same way, the dialectic of the dual narrative paradoxically offers both an enactment and a critique of the sexual division into separate spheres. At one level, it enacts it by leading to a conventionally happy ending for the heroine/narrator Esther, which comes to her as a reward for proper "womanly" behaviour. But at another level it deconstructs itself by signally failing to contain the violence it apparently seeks to repress but in fact covertly fosters. This violence, simmering underground throughout the novel, erupts at intervals until it is finally appeased by the cathartic end of Lady Dedlock. Thus Esther's reward can only come at the expense of the destruction of her mother, who takes on all the "sins" of illicit female sexuality which so threaten the fabric of a patrilineal society. Surely this is what still sticks in the throat about the character of Esther, after all the psychological explanations have been accepted; she is rewarded for having purged her mother's sexual taint, and by so doing, for having connived at what amounts to her own clitoridectomy.

Chronology

1812	Charles John Huffam Dickens, the second of eight children, is born February 7 to John and Elizabeth Dickens.
1814	John Dickens, a clerk in the Navy Pay Office, is transferred from Portsea to London. During these early years, from 1814 to 1821, Dickens is taught his letters by his mother, and he immerses himself in the fiction classics of his father's library.
1817	John Dickens moves family to Chatham.
1821	Dickens begins school with the son of a Baptist minister; he remains at this school for a time even after his family is transferred again to London in 1822.
1824	John Dickens is arrested for debt and sent to Marshalsea Prison, accompanied by his wife and younger children. Charles soon finds lodging in a poor neighborhood and begins work at Warren's Blacking Factory. His father is released three months later and Charles returns to school.
1824–26	Dickens attends Wellington House Academy, London.
1827	Works as a law clerk and spends time reading in the British Museum.
1830	Meets Maria Beadnell; he eventually falls in love with her, but she jilts him upon return from a trip to Paris in 1833.
1831	Becomes a reporter for the *Mirror of Parliament*.
1832	Becomes a staffwriter for the *True Sun*.
1833	Dickens's first published piece, "A Dinner at Poplar Walk," appears in a December issue of the *Monthly Magazine* under the pen name "Boz."
1834	Dickens becomes a staff writer on the *Morning Chronicle*. His "street sketches" begin to appear in the *Evening*

	Chronicle. Dickens meets his future wife, Catherine Hogarth. Also, John Dickens is arrested again for debt.
1836	*Sketches by Boz,* illustrated by George Cruikshank, published. Dickens marries Catherine Hogarth in April. Also in this year, his first play, *The Strange Gentleman,* runs for two months at the St. James's Theatre. A second play, *The Village Coquettes,* is produced at the same theatre. Dickens meets John Forster, who becomes a lifelong friend and his biographer.
1836–37	*Pickwick Papers* published in monthly installments from April through the following November.
1837	*Pickwick Papers* appears in book form. *Oliver Twist* begins to appear in *Bentley's Miscellany. Is She His Wife?* produced at the St. James's. Dickens's first child born, and the family moves to Doughty Street. Catherine's sister Mary, deeply loved by Dickens, dies suddenly.
1838	*Nicholas Nickleby* appears in installments; completed in October of 1839. Dickens's first daughter born.
1839	The Dickenses move to Devonshire Terrace. A second daughter born. *Nickleby* appears in book form.
1840	Dickens edits *Master Humphrey's Clock,* a weekly periodical, in which *The Old Curiosity Shop* appears.
1841	*Barnaby Rudge* appears in *Master Humphrey's Clock.* Another son born.
1842	Dickens and his wife tour America from January to June; Dickens publishes *American Notes* and begins *Martin Chuzzlewit.*
1843	*Martin Chuzzlewit* appears in monthly installments (January 1843–July 1844). *A Christmas Carol* published.
1844	Dickens tours Italy and Switzerland. Another Christmas book, *The Chimes,* completed. A third son born.
1845	Dickens produces *Every Man in his Humour* in England. *The Cricket on the Hearth* is written by Christmas, and Dickens begins *Pictures from Italy.* A fourth son born.
1846	Dickens creates and edits the *Daily News,* but resigns as editor after seventeen days. Begins *Dombey and Son* while in Lausanne; the novel appears in twenty monthly installments (October 1846–April 1848). *The Battle of Life: A Love Story* appears for Christmas.
1847	Dickens begins to manage a theatrical company and ar-

ranges a benefit tour of *Every Man in his Humour*. Fifth son born.

1848   Daughter Fanny dies. Dickens's theatrical company performs for Queen Victoria. It also performs *The Merry Wives of Windsor* to raise money for the preservation of Shakespeare's birthplace. Dickens's last Christmas book, *The Haunted Man*, published.

1849   Dickens begins *David Copperfield* (published May 1849–November 1850). A sixth son born.

1850   *Household Words*, a weekly periodical, established with Dickens as editor. A third daughter born who dies within a year.

1851   Dickens and his company participate in theatrical fund-raising. Dickens's father dies.

1852   *Bleak House* appears in monthly installments (March 1852–September 1853). The first bound volume of *A Child's History of England* appears. The Dickens's last child, their seventh son, born.

1853   Dickens gives first public readings, from the Christmas books. Travels to France and Italy.

1854   *Hard Times* published in *Household Words* (April 1–August 12) and appears in book form.

1855   *Little Dorrit* appears in monthly installments (December 1855–June 1857). Dickens and family travel at year's end to Paris, where the novelist meets other leading literary and theatrical persons.

1856   Dickens purchases Gad's Hill Place, and the family returns to London.

1857   Dickens is involved primarily with theatrical productions.

1858   Dickens announces his separation from his wife, about which he writes a personal statement in *Household Words*.

1859   Dickens concludes *Household Words* and establishes a new weekly, *All the Year Round*. *A Tale of Two Cities* appears there from April 20 to November 26, and is published in book form in December.

1860   *Great Expectations* underway in weekly installments (December 1860–August 1861).

1861   *The Uncommercial Traveller*, a collection of pieces from *All the Year Round*, published.

1862   Dickens gives many public readings and travels to Paris.

1863   Dickens continues his readings in Paris and London. Daughter Elizabeth dies.

1864   *Our Mutual Friend* appears in monthly installments for publisher Chapman and Hall (May 1864–November 1865).

1865   Dickens suffers a stroke that leaves him lame. Involved in train accident, which causes him to change the ending of *Our Mutual Friend*. *Our Mutual Friend* appears in book form. The second collection of *The Uncommercial Traveller* published.

1866   Dickens gives thirty public readings in the English provinces.

1867   Continues the provincial readings, then travels to America in November, where he reads in Boston and New York. This tour permanently breaks the novelist's health.

1868   In April, Dickens returns to England, where he continues to tour.

1869   The first public reading of the murder of Nancy (from *Oliver Twist*) performed, but Dickens's doctors recommend he discontinue the tour. *The Mystery of Edwin Drood* begun.

1870   Dickens gives twelve readings in London. Six parts of *Edwin Drood* appear from April to September. On June 9, Charles Dickens dies, aged 58. He is buried in the Poets' Corner, Westminster Abbey.

Contributors

HAROLD BLOOM, Sterling Professor of the Humanities at Yale University, is the author of *The Anxiety of Influence, Poetry and Repression* and many other volumes of literary criticism. His forthcoming study, *Freud: Transference and Authority*, attempts a full-scale reading of all of Freud's major works. He is the general editor of five series of literary criticism published by Chelsea House. During 1987–88, he was appointed Charles Eliot Norton Professor of Poetry at Harvard University.

J. HILLIS MILLER is Professor of English at the University of California, Irvine. He is best known as a spokesman for both the Geneva school of criticism of Georges Poulet and the deconstruction of Jacques Derrida and the late Paul de Man. His studies of Victorian and modern literature include *The Disappearance of God, Poets of Reality* and important books on Charles Dickens and Thomas Hardy. He has also written extensively on William Carlos Williams and Wallace Stevens.

ALEX ZWERDLING is Professor of English at the University of California, Berkeley. He has published on Virginia Woolf.

JUDITH WILT is Professor of English at Boston College. She is the author of *Ghosts of the Gothic: Austen, Eliot and Lawrence, The Readable People of George Meredith* and *Secret Leaves: The Novels of Walter Scott*.

GARRETT STEWART teaches at the University of California, Santa Barbara. He has published two books: *Death Sentences: Styles of Dying in British Fiction* and *Dickens and the Trials of Imagination*.

JOHN KUCICH is Associate Professor of English at the University of Michigan. He is the author of *Excess and Restraint in the Novels of Charles Dickens*.

161

CHRISTOPHER HERBERT is Associate Professor of English at Northwestern University. He has published on George Eliot, Dickens, De Quincey and Eliza Lynn Linton. He is currently working on a study of Trollope.

VIRGINIA BLAIN is Senior Lecturer at Macquarie University, Australia. She has published on Virginia Woolf and is the editor of R. S. Surtees's *Mr. Sponge's Sporting Tour*.

Bibliography

Axton, William. "Dickens Now." In *The Victorian Experience: The Novelists.* Edited by Richard A. Levine, 19–48. Athens: Ohio University Press, 1976.

———. "The Trouble with Esther." *Modern Language Quarterly* 26 (1965): 545–57.

Boege, Fred W. "Point of View in Dickens." *PMLA* 65 (1950): 90–105.

Brice, A. W., and K. J. Fielding. "*Bleak House* and the Graveyard." In *Dickens the Craftsman: Strategies of Presentation,* edited by Robert B. Partlow, Jr. Carbondale: Southern Illinois University Press, 1970.

Butt, John. "*Bleak House* in the Context of 1851." *Nineteenth-Century Fiction* 10 (1955): 1–21.

Butt, John, and Kathleen Tillotson. *Dickens at Work.* London: Methuen, 1957.

Carey, John. *The Violent Effigy: A Study of Dickens's Imagination.* London: Faber & Faber, 1973.

Chesterton, G. K. *Charles Dickens.* London: Methuen, 1906.

Churchill, R. C., comp. and ed. *Bibliography of Dickensian Criticism 1836–1975.* New York: Garland, 1975.

Cohan, Steven. " 'They Are All Secret': The Fantasy Content of *Bleak House.*" *Literature and Psychology* 26, no. 2 (1976): 79–91.

Collins, Philip. *A Critical Commentary on Dickens's* Bleak House. London: Macmillan, 1971.

———. *Dickens and Crime.* London: Macmillan, 1962.

———, ed. *Dickens: The Critical Heritage.* London: Routledge & Kegan Paul, 1971.

Daleski, H. M. *Dickens and the Art of Analogy.* New York: Shocken, 1970.

Davis, Robert Con, ed. *The Fictional Father: Lacanian Readings of the Text.* Amherst: University of Massachusetts Press, 1981.

Dickens Studies Annual: Essays in Victorian Fiction. Vols. 1–7 (1970–78), Carbondale: Southern Illinois University Press. Vols. 8–13 (1980–85), New York: AMS Press.

Dickens Studies Newsletter, 1970–83. Changed to *Dickens Quarterly,* 1984–.

Dickensian, The, 1905–.

Dyson, A. E. *The Inimitable Dickens: A Reading of the Novels.* London: Macmillan, 1970.

Fenstermaker, John J. *Charles Dickens, 1940–1975: An Analytical Subject Index to Periodical Criticism of the Novels and Christmas Books.* Boston: G. K. Hall, 1979.

Ford, George H. *Dickens and His Readers: Aspects of Novel Criticism since 1836.*

Princeton: Princeton Universtiy Press, 1955.

Ford, George H., and Lauriat Lane, Jr., eds. *The Dickens Critics*. Ithaca: Cornell University Press, 1961.

Forster, John. *The Life of Charles Dickens*. Edited by A. J. Hoppe. 2 vols. London: Dent, 1966.

Garis, Robert E. *The Dickens Theatre: A Reassessment of the Novels*. Oxford: Clarendon, 1965.

Grenander, M. E. "The Mystery and the Moral: Point of View in Dickens's *Bleak House*." *Nineteenth-Century Fiction* 9 (1956): 301–5.

Hardy, Barbara. *The Moral Art of Dickens*. New York: Oxford University Press, 1970.

Hirsch, Gordon D. "The Mysteries in *Bleak House:* A Psychoanalytic Study." *Dickens Studies Annual* 4 (1975): 132–52.

House, Humphry. *The Dickens World*. London: Oxford University Press, 1941.

Johnson, Edgar. *Charles Dickens: His Tragedy and Triumph*. New York: Simon and Schuster, 1952.

Kaplan, Fred. *Dickens and Mesmerism*. Princeton: Princeton University Press, 1975.

Kennedy, Valerie. "*Bleak House:* More Trouble with Esther?" *Journal of Women's Studies in Literature* 1 (Autumn 1979): 330–47.

Kettle, Arnold. "Balzac and Dickens." In *The Modern World, II: Realities,* edited by David Daiches and Anthony Thorlby, 239–66. London: Aldus Books, 1972.

LaCapra, Dominick. "Ideology and Critique in Dickens's *Bleak House*." *Representations* 6 (Spring 1984): 116–23.

Leavis, F. R., and Q. D. Leavis. *Dickens the Novelist*. London: Chatto & Windus, 1970.

Lerner, Laurence. *Love and Marriage: Literature and Its Social Context*. London: Edward Arnold, 1979.

Levy, Diane Wolfe. "Dickens's *Bleak House*." *Explicator* 38 (Spring 1980): 40–42.

———. "Under Capricorn." *Representations* 6 (Spring 1984): 124–29.

Miller, D. A. "Discipline in Different Voices: Bureaucracy, Police, Family, and *Bleak House*." *Representations* 11, no. 1 (February 1983): 59–89.

Moers, Ellen. "*Bleak House:* The Agitating Women." *The Dickensian* 69 (1973): 13–29.

Monod, Sylvère. *Dickens the Novelist*. Norman: University of Oklahoma Press, 1968.

Morton, Lionel. "Allegories of Silence: Dickens's Use of the Word 'Allegory.' " *English Studies in Canada* 4 (Winter 1978): 430–49.

Nabokov, Vladimir. "*Bleak House* (1852–1853)." In *Lectures on Literature,* edited by Fredson Bowers. New York: Harcourt Brace Jovanovich, 1980.

Newsom, Robert. *Dickens on the Romantic Side of Familiar Things:* Bleak House *and the Novel Tradition*. New York: Columbia University Press, 1977.

Orwell, George. "Charles Dickens." In *Dickens, Dali and Others: Studies in Popular Culture,* 1–75. New York: Reynal and Hitchcock, 1946.

Ousby, Ian. "The Broken Glass: Vision and Comprehension in *Bleak House*." *Nineteenth-Century Fiction* 29 (March 1975): 381–92.

Parker, Dorothy. "Allegory and the Extension of Mr. Bucket's Forefinger." *English Language Notes* 12 (Sept. 1974): 31–35.

Pei, Lowry. "Mirrors, the Dead Child, Snagsby's Secret, and Esther." *English Language Notes* 16 (December 1978): 144–56.

Quirk, Eugene F. "Tulkinghorn's Buried Life: A Study of Character in *Bleak House*." *Journal of English and Germanic Philology* 72 (1972): 526–35.

Scott, P. J. M. *Reality and Comic Confidence in Charles Dickens*. London: Macmillan, 1979.

Senf, Carol A. "*Bleak House:* Dickens, Esther, and the Androgynous Mind." *The Victorian Newsletter* 64 (Fall 1983): 21–27.

Serlen, Ellen. "The Two Worlds of *Bleak House*." *ELH* 43 (Winter 1976): 551–66.

Smith, Grahame. *Charles Dickens:* Bleak House. Studies in English Literature 54. London: Edward Arnold, 1974.

Steele, Peter. "Dickens and the Grotesque." *Quadrant* 17 (Mar.–Apr. 1973): 15–23.

Steig, Michael. "Structure and the Grotesque in Dickens: *Dombey and Son, Bleak House*." *Centennial Review* 14 (Summer 1970): 313–31.

Steig, Michael, and F. A. C. Wilson. "Hortense versus Bucket: The Ambiguity of Order in *Bleak House*." *Modern Language Quarterly* 33 (1972): 289–98.

Stoehr, Taylor. *Dickens: The Dreamer's Stance*. Ithaca: Cornell University Press, 1965.

Stone, Donald D. *The Romantic Impulse in Victorian Fiction*. Cambridge: Harvard University Press, 1980.

Sucksmith, Harvey Peter. *The Narrative Art of Charles Dickens: The Rhetoric of Sympathy and Irony in His Novels*. Oxford: Clarendon, 1970.

Thurley, Geoffrey. *Dickens's Mythology*. New York: St. Martin's, 1976.

Van Ghent, Dorothy. "The Dickens World: A View from Todgers's." *Sewanee Review* 58 (1950): 419–38.

Wilson, Angus. *The World of Charles Dickens*. New York: Viking, 1970.

Acknowledgments

"The Interpretive Dance in *Bleak House*" (originally entitled "Introduction") by J. Hillis Miller from *Bleak House* by Charles Dickens, edited by Norman Paige, © 1971 by Penguin Books Ltd. Reprinted by permission.

"Esther Summerson Rehabilitated" by Alex Zwerdling from *PMLA* 88, no. 3 (May 1973), © 1973 by the Modern Language Association of America. Reprinted by permission of the Modern Language Association of America.

"Confusion and Consciousness in Dicken's Esther" by Judith Wilt from *Nineteenth Century Fiction* 32, no. 3 (December 1977), © 1977 by the Regents of the University of California. Reprinted by permission of the University of California Press.

"Epitaphic Chapter Titles and the New Mortality of *Bleak House*" (originally entitled "The New Mortality of *Bleak House*") by Garrett Stewart from *ELH* 45, no. 3 (Fall 1978), © 1978 by the Johns Hopkins University Press, Baltimore/London. Reprinted by permission.

"Endings" by John Kucich from *Excess and Restraint in the Novels of Charles Dickens* by John Kucich, © 1981 by the University of Georgia Press. Reprinted by permission.

"The Occult in *Bleak House*" by Christopher Herbert from *Novel: A Forum on Fiction* 17, no. 2 (Winter 1984), © 1984 by Novel Corporation. Reprinted by permission.

"Double Vision and the Double Standard in *Bleak House*: A Feminist Perspective" by Virginia Blain from *Literature and History* 11, no. 1 (Spring 1985), © 1985 by Thames Polytechnic. Reprinted by permission.

Index

169